Landmarks of world literature

James Boswell

THE LIFE OF JOHNSON

JAMES BOSWELL

The Life of Johnson

GREG CLINGHAM

Department of English,
Fordham University, New York

Published by the Press Syndicate of the University of Cambridge
The Pitt Building, Trumpington Street, Cambridge CB2 1RP
40 West 20th Street, New York NY 10011-4211, USA
10 Stamford Road, Oakleigh, Victoria 3166, Australia

© Cambridge University Press 1992

First published 1992

Printed in Great Britain at the University Press, Cambridge

A catalogue record for this book is available from the British Library

Library of Congress cataloguing in publication data

Clingham, Greg.
James Boswell: the Life of Johnson / Greg Clingham.
    p.   cm. − (Landmarks of world literature)
ISBN 0 521 37304 2 (hardback)
1. Boswell, James, 1740−1795. Life of Johnson.   2. Authors,
English − Biography − History and criticism.   3. Johnson, Samuel,
1709−1784 − Biography.   4. Biography (as a literary form)   I. Title.
II. Series.
PR3533.B7C57   1992
828'.609 − dc20   91-43819   CIP

ISBN 0 521 37304 2 hardback

WG

Contents

vi   Contents

Preface

This book was written with the financial assistance of a National Endowment for the Humanities Summer Fellowship, a short-term Fellowship at the William Andrews Clark Memorial Library, and a Fordham University Faculty Research grant.

Modest as this book is I have incurred many debts in completing it, and it is a pleasure to acknowledge them. I am generally indebted to Philip Davis's *In Mind of Johnson* (London, 1989). J.P. Stern read two versions in manuscript and made many challenging comments that helped focus my arguments. I have benefited from the generous and stimulating conversation of Marc Ricciardi. The staff at the Clark Library (and some of its readers during my tenure) made my stay here happy and fruitful. Sue Owen helped clarify some issues in relation to Boswell and sexual politics. Margaret Mary Sullivan, in the course of one conversation over two glasses of beer, taught me something essential about Boswell which I had not seen in all the books I had read. My editors at Cambridge University Press, Kevin Taylor and Kate Brett, were supportive throughout.

I have learnt invaluable things pertaining to the subject(s) of this book from Linda Lou Schoeman, from the people at the New York Healing Circle, especially from my late friend John Fletcher Harris, and from the people at the Corlears School ACOA meeting in New York. With great pleasure I acknowledge three particular friends in Los Angeles for their wit, affection, and support while I was writing this book — and for the difference they made: Marina Romani, Clare Spark, and Lisa Worksman. Finally I'd like to dedicate this work to my friend Shari Cordon whose affection and tenderness helped me often to turn difficulty into discovery and frustration into a kind of freedom.

Textual note

The edition of the *Life of Johnson* quoted from in this book is that in the Oxford World's Classics series, edited by R.W. Chapman (corrected by J.D. Fleeman), with an introduction by Pat Rogers (1980). I wish to acknowledge the permission of Oxford University Press to use their text. The *Journal of a Tour to the Hebrides* is quoted from the Penguin edition (1984), edited with an introduction and notes by Peter Levi. When quoting from the *London Journal, 1762–3* I have used the paperback edition (1968) of F.A. Pottle's standard Yale text (1950), now republished by Edinburgh University Press (1991). And in quoting from the *Account of Corsica* (for which there is no edition in print) I have used the first edition (Glasgow, 1769).

Chronology

	Boswell's life	Historical events	Literary events
1738			Johnson, 'London'
1740	JB born in Edinburgh 29 October, first son of Alexander Boswell and Euphemia Erskine		
1740–1			Richardson, *Pamela*; Hume, *Treatise of Human Nature* (vol. I, 1739); Fielding, *Shamela*
1740–8		War of Spanish Succession	
1742		Walpole resigns as Prime Minister	Pope, *New Dunciad*; Young, *Night Thoughts* (concl. 1746); Fielding, *Joseph Andrews*
1743			Blair, *The Grave*
1744		Pelham ministry; France declares war on Britain	Johnson, 'Life of Savage'; Akenside, *Pleasures of the Imagination*
1745–6		Jacobite uprisings in Scotland; Charles Edward Stuart ('Bonnie Prince Charlie') defeated at Culloden – subjugation of Scottish Highlands	
c. 1746–9	Attends Mundell's private school, Edinburgh		
1747–8			Richardson, *Clarissa*
1748		Peace of Aix-la-Chapelle	Montesquieu, *Spirit of the Laws*; Smollet, *Roderick Random*

	Boswell's life	Historical events	Literary events
1749	AB succeeds to family estate of Auchinleck, Ayrshire		Johnson, 'Vanity of Human Wishes'; Fielding, *Tom Jones*; Bolingbroke, *Idea of a Patriot King*
1750–2			Johnson, *The Rambler*
1751		Gin Act	Voltaire, *Age of Louis XIV*; Gray, 'Elegy wrote in a Country Churchyard'; Hume, *Enquiry Concerning Principles of Morals*
1752		Reform of the calendar in Britain	
1753–9	JB at Edinburgh University		
1754	AB appointed judge of Court of Session, takes title of Lord Auchinleck	Newcastle ministry; Anglo-French War begins in North America	Hume, *History of Great Britain* (concl. 1763)
1755	Lord Auchinleck appointed judge of Court of Justiciary	Lisbon earthquake	Johnson, *Dictionary*; Rousseau, *Discourse on Inequality*
1756–63		Seven Years' War	
1757		Coalition of Pitt and Newcastle	Gray, *Odes*; Home, *Douglas*; Smollett, *History of England* (concl. 1765)
1758	*October, a Poem*, first published work		
1758–60			Johnson, *The Idler*
1759			Johnson, *Rasselas*; Voltaire, *Candide*; Young, 'Conjectures on Original Composition'
1759–60	JB at Glasgow University		
1760	Runs away to London	Accession of George III	Macpherson ('Ossian'), *Fragments of Ancient Poetry*; Sterne, *Tristram Shandy* (concl. 1767)
1760–2	Studies law in Edinburgh		

1762	*Collection of Original Poems by Scotch Gentlemen*, containing 31 poems by JB; Johnson's pension	Bute ministry	Rousseau, *Social Contract* and *Emile*; Diderot, *Rameau's Nephew*; Kames, *Elements of Criticism*
1762–3	JB in London, writing *London Journal*		
1763	*Letters between the Honourable Andrew Erskine and James Boswell, Esq*; JB meets Johnson (16 May)	Grenville succeeds Bute; Wilkes publishes No. 45 of the *North Briton* and is arrested for seditious libel	Blair, 'Dissertation on Ossian'
1763–4	Studies law at Utrecht		
1764		Wilkes expelled from House of Commons	Voltaire, *Philosophical Dictionary*; Goldsmith, 'The Traveller'
1764–6	On the Grand Tour of Germany, Switzerland, Italy, Corsica, and France (meets Rousseau, Voltaire, Pascal Paoli)		
1765		Stamp Act (to tax American Colonies); Rockingham ministry	Percy, *Reliques of Ancient Poetry*; Blackstone, *Commentaries on the Laws of England* (concl. 1769); Johnson's edition of Shakespeare
1766	JB's mother dies; JB advocate at Scots Bar (29 July); Rousseau in England	Stamp Act repealed; Grafton–Pitt ministry	Goldsmith, *Vicar of Wakefield*
1767	*Dorando; Essence of the Douglas Cause; Letters of Lady Jane Douglas*	Taxes on tea in America; Grafton forms ministry	
1768	*An Account of Corsica*	Wilkes sentenced for libel; Corsica ceded to France	Sterne, *Sentimental Journey*
1769	Paoli exiled in London; JB marries Margaret Montgomery, a first cousin, in Ayrshire. Lord Auchinleck marries his first cousin, Elizabeth Boswell, in Edinburgh	Wilkes expelled from Commons; re-elected three times	

	Boswell's life	Historical events	Literary events
1770		North ministry; printers and publishers of *Junius* tried for seditious libel	Goldsmith, 'Deserted Village'; Burke, *Thoughts on the Present Discontents*; Johnson, 'The False Alarm' Smollet, *Humphrey Clinker*
1771	Paoli visits Scotland		
1772	JB in London for first time since marriage	Warren Hastings governor of Bengal	
1773	JB's daughter Veronica born; JB elected to Johnson's Club; tours Highlands and Hebrides with Johnson	Boston 'tea party'	
1774	JB's second daughter, Euphemia, born; JB defends John Reid, sheep-stealer	First Congress of American Colonies; accession of Louis XVI in France	Burke, 'Speech on American Taxation'; Thomas Warton, *History of English Poetry* (concl. 1781)
1775	JB's first son, Alexander, born	Battles of Lexington, Concord, and Bunker Hill; Watt's steam engine perfected	Johnson, *Journey to the Western Isles of Scotland* and 'Taxation No Tyranny'
1776		American Declaration of Independence	Hawkins, *History of Music*; Smith, *Wealth of Nations* Chatterton, *Poems ... by Rowley*; Hume, 'Life, Written by Himself'; Robertson, *History of America*
1777	With Johnson for 10 days, at Ashbourne, Derbyshire (September)		
1777–83	*The Hypochondriack*		
1778	JB's second son, James, born	Franco–American alliance formed; Britain declares war on France	Frances Burney, *Evelina*
1779		War with Spain	
1779–81			Hume, *Dialogues Concerning Natural Religion* Johnson, *Prefaces, Biographical and Critical, to the Works of the English Poets* (*Lives of the Poets*)
1780	JB's third daughter, Elizabeth, born	Gordon Riots	

Year			
1781		Cornwallis defeated at Yorktown	Kant, *Critique of Pure Reason* Frances Burney, *Cecilia*
1782	Lord Auchinleck dies (30 August). JB succeeds as Laird of Auchinleck	North succeeded by Rockingham and then Shelburn; Burke's 'economical reform'; Ireland's legislative independence; French fleet defeated	
1783	First *Letter to the People of Scotland, On the Present State of the Nation* (on Fox's East India Bill)	Fox–North coalition, followed by Pitt the Younger's first ministry	Blake, *Poetical Sketches*; Crabbe, 'The Village'; Blair, *Lectures on Rhetoric and Belles Lettres*
1784	Johnson dies (13 December)	Pitt's India Act	
1785	Second *Letter to the People of Scotland* (on the bill to diminish the number of Lords of Session); *Journal of a Tour to the Hebrides*; JB meets Lord Lonsdale	Warren Hastings returns from India; Cartwright invents power loom	Cowper, *The Task*; Johnson, *Prayers and Meditations*
1786	Called to the English Bar (13 February)		Burns, *Poems Chiefly in the Scottish Dialect*; Piozzi, *Anecdotes of Samuel Johnson* Hawkins, *Life of Samuel Johnson*
1787		United States Constitution signed; Association for Abolition of Slave Trade begins	
1788	Appointed Recorder of Carlisle by Lonsdale Margaret dies (4 June)	French States-General summoned; impeachment of Warren Hastings	
1789		Fall of Bastille; Declaration of the Rights of Man; Pitt Prime Minister; French National Assembly	Blake, *Songs of Innocence* and *Book of Thel*
1790	Breaks with Lonsdale, resigns Recordership		Blake, *Marriage of Heaven and Hell*; Burke, *Reflections on the Revolution in France*
1791	*No Abolition of Slavery; the Universal Empire of Love*; *Life of Samuel Johnson, LL.D.* (16 May)		Paine, *Rights of Man*

	Boswell's life	Historical events	Literary events
1792		Imprisonment of Louis XVI; Austria declares war on France; Warren Hastings acquitted	Wollstonecraft, *Vindication of the Rights of Woman*
1793	Second edition of *Life*	Trial and execution of Louis XVI; the 'Terror'	Godwin, *Political Justice*
1795	JB dies in London (19 May)		

Some of the principal scenes and conversations in the 'Life'

Date and page nos.	(1) Place and people present (2) Subjects of conversation
16 6 Oct. 1769; 407–9	JB at Streatham for first time.
17 10 Oct. 1769; 409–10	(1) SJ meets Pascal Paoli in London. (2) Languages.
18 16 Oct. 1769; 411–19	(1) Dinner at JB's lodgings, Old Bond Street. SJ, JB, Reynolds, Garrick, Goldsmith, Murphy, Bickerstaff, Davies. (2) Garrick's playfulness, Goldsmith's histrionics, Dryden's and Congreve's drama compared to Shakespeare's, executions, sympathy, comic theatre, politics, cultural issues.
19 26 Oct. 1769; 419–27	(1) SJ and JB dine at Mitre, tea with Mrs Williams. (2) Catholicism, Presbyterianism, predestination, purgatory and other Catholic doctrines, Hume and fear of death, Mrs Williams's tea-making, JB asking whimsical questions, natural affection, habits.
20 21 Mar. 1772; 459–65	(1) JB, Mrs Williams, Mrs Desmoulins, Stockdale in SJ's study. (2) JB's legal defence of schoolmaster, Scottish politics, Church of Scotland, 'second sight', Catholicism, 39 Articles, English politics, 'mimickry'.
21 30 April 1773; 527–31	(1) Lord Charlemont, Reynolds, SJ, JB, other members of the Club at Beauclerk's. (2) Goldsmith's and Robertson's histories, Bunyan, *Whole Duty of Man*, JB elected to Club.
22 7 May 1773; 537–45	(1) Edward Dilly, Goldsmith, Langton, Claxton, Mayo, Toplady, Temple, SJ, JB at Charles Dilly's and at Club. (2) Hawkesworth on South Seas, birds, difference between animals and humans, toleration and order, martyrdom, education, the Trinity, convocation of Saints, (Goldsmith's tantrums and desire for conspicuousness).
23 10 May 1773; 548–9	SJ laughs at Langton having his will made by Chambers. [SJ and JB in Scotland, 18 Aug. to 22 Nov. 1773]
24 1 April 1775; 602–3	SJ 'scraping oranges'.
25 18 April 1775; 625–32	(1) Reynolds, SJ, JB, at Owen Cambridge's villa near Twickenham. (2) Painting, humour, SJ's *Journey to Western Islands*, Walton's Lives, history, *Beggar's Opera*, Sheridan's marriage to a singer, modern politics, *Hubridas* and Restoration politics, *Spectator* and Sir Roger de Coverley, (SJ's 'promptitude of argument').
26 16 Mar. 1776; 680–8	(1) Mrs Thrale, JB at SJ's home, Bolt Court, and then SJ and JB crossing Thames to Blackfriars. (2) Macleods, entails, *Wealth of Nations*, militia bill for Scotland, story-telling and truth, drinking, education.

Chapter 1

Boswell's reputation

'Obviously, no book can replace Boswell's. Boswell's thorough-
ness, his skill in re-creating the everyday drama of Johnson's
life, and the easy, familiar style which graces his entire book,
have rightly lifted his *Life of Johnson* to a position of supremacy
among works of its kind.' These are the words of Bertram
Davis, introducing the biography of Johnson not by Boswell,
but by Sir John Hawkins, one of Boswell's main contemporary
rivals (Hawkins xxvii). Since the time of Macaulay and Carlyle,
Davis's view of Boswell has been widespread: he has been
regarded as the greatest biographer in English, and he has
received attention of the kind effectively to supplant Johnson
in the popular mind and in the estimation of many students of
eighteenth-century literature. What constitutes the originality
and power of the *Life of Johnson*, first published two hundred
years ago, in 1791?

The *Life* stands in several important literary traditions
that would require explication in a full-scale discussion of
its origins. Most immediately, the *Life* stands in the native
English tradition of biography, including such works as
the Lives of Cowley by Sprat (1668), of Gray by Mason
(1748), of Cicero by Middleton (1750), and Johnson's *Lives
of the Poets* (1779–81). Behind the newly developing genre
of biography in the eighteenth century lies the equally important sub-genre of the biographical mini-portrait (epitomised
by Clarendon's portraits of political and literary figures
in his *History of the Rebellion* and the *Life by Himself*),
and of puritan autobiography, represented by Bunyan's
Pilgrim's Progress and the novels of Daniel Defoe and Samuel
Richardson. In these traditions Boswell would have discovered the basics of eighteenth-century biography, and
also found examples of blending confessional with novelistic

characteristics, and biographical with autobiographical. One
of the works of the European Enlightenment to which Boswell
has a complex relation is Rousseau's *Confessions* (1782–9)
as well as to his other autobiographical works. As a young
man Boswell read Rousseau's *Emile* and *Nouvelle Heloise*
avidly, interviewed Rousseau in 1764 while on his Grand
Tour of Europe, and both writers were deeply concerned
with the inter-relationships of autobiographical writing, self-
discovery, truth, freedom, and justice.

At the same time, Boswell's *Life of Johnson* stands in the
European tradition of table-talk. It is impossible to demonstrate
direct influences on Boswell, but the abundant miscellaneous
detail of Johnson's talk in the *Life* is anticipated in such
works as *The Familiar Discourses of Dr Martin Luther at
His Table* (1652) and John Selden's *Table Talk* (1689), and
it is echoed later in William Hazlitt's *The Round Table* (1817)
and *Table Talk* (1821–2), S.T. Coleridge's *Table Talk* published by H.N. Coleridge in 1835, and, more significantly,
in Johann Eckermann's *Conversations with Goethe* (1836).
Boswell's work shares with these memoirs and collections of
ana a knowledge that true table-talk, far from being common
chat, is informal discourse suited to all the personal, intellectual,
civic circumstances of the hearers, yet the *Life* is a landmark
for additional reasons.

It does certain things that no other previous biography does:
by use of Johnson's letters and other personal documents, by
the assimilation of information provided by many people who
had known Johnson, by the assiduous and minute attention
to and selection of detail, and, especially, by a dramatic
rendition of Johnson's conversation, Boswell creates the
impression of the presence and life of a real person. Boswell
considered his biographical method a 'perfect mode of writing
any man's life' because it enabled the reader to 'see him
[Johnson] live, and to "live o'er each scene" with him, as he
actually advanced through the several stages of his life' (22).

The success of Boswell's intention was soon acknowledged
in the 1790s, and confirmed by the reviews of later editions by
Lord Macaulay (1831) and Thomas Carlyle (1832). Macaulay's

review of Croker's edition of the *Life*, and his later 'Life of Johnson' for the Encyclopedia Britannica (1856), has done more than any other later work to enforce the opinion that Johnson lives for, and is interesting to posterity by virtue of Boswell's presentation, rather than by his own artistic volition:

> Since [Johnson's] death, the popularity of his works ... has greatly diminished. But though the celebrity of his writings may have declined, the celebrity of the writer, strange to say, is as great as ever. Boswell's book has done for him more than the best of his own books could do. The memory of other authors is kept alive by their works. But the memory of Johnson keeps many of his works alive. The old philosopher is still among us in the brown coat with metal buttons, and the shirt which ought to be at wash, blinking, puffing, rolling his head, drumming with his fingers, tearing his meat like a tiger, and swallowing his tea in oceans. No human being who has been more than seventy years in the grave is so well known to us.
>
> (Arnold 41–2)

Modern opinion has silently accepted and echoed these views: the detail, the dramatic scenes and conversations, the range of characters from literary, social, political, and London life, the vividness of Boswell's narrative have convinced readers that the *Life* is among the definitive representations of eighteenth-century life and of who Samuel Johnson was. At the same time the effectiveness of the *Life* has convinced readers of the possibility of understanding Johnson fully without taking into consideration his works. The logic of these phenomena and the nature of Boswell's biography are essential to what make the work a landmark.

Chapter 2

Boswell's art in the *Life*

Our understanding of the *Life* has been radically shaped by the discovery (and the subsequent deposit in Yale University Library) of Boswell's private papers at Malahide Castle and Fettercairn House in 1925–6 and 1930–1 (see *LJ*, Preface for John Morley's account of the discoveries). The privately published edition of the papers by Geoffrey Scott and F. A. Pottle (18 vols., 1928–34), the selection in thirteen volumes as part of the Yale Editions of the Private Papers of James Boswell (1950–89), together with Marshall Waingrow's edition of the *Correspondence and Other Papers Relating to the Making of the Life of Johnson* (as part of the 'research edition'), have made it possible for scholars to witness Boswell's creativity, his relation to his own practice of composition, and to begin to understand that the *Life of Johnson*, far from being autonomous and monolithic, is an integral part of Boswell's life and other journalistic and autobiographical writings.

Geoffrey Scott and F. A. Pottle's recognition that the *Life* is based on and composed from a myriad of memoranda and journal entries characteristic of Boswell's lifelong habit of recording his relationships with the world and his search for self helps us to rethink the genesis of the *Life* and to appreciate Boswell's artistry in constructing it. It also indicates that his personal relationship with his material and with his images of Samuel Johnson is essential to the *Life* as biography. Boswell's representation of Johnson, however, has become entangled with theoretical arguments over the nature of biography, and with the unacknowledged battle over who possesses the 'true' or 'real' Johnson. Boswell documents this battle (between Johnson's friends) in the *Life*, and he extends it by setting up Hawkins and Mrs Thrale as his biographical rivals. These are arguments that need to be clarified at the beginning of a discussion of the *Life of Johnson* as biography.

Critics agree that Boswell is a great biographer because he is a great artist, but Boswellians mean something very particular by this. While it is known that Boswell did not and could not simply transcribe Johnson's conversation, critics take two attitudes towards Boswell's artifice. Some, such as Rader, Dowling, and Bogel, take Boswell's dramatic artifice and fictional techniques for granted, and see the *Life* as self-contained, self-consistent, and self-reflexive. Others, such as Pottle, Brady, Scott, and Waingrow, also admire Boswell's dramatising powers, but claim in addition that his presentation of Johnson is factually accurate and authentic. By themselves Boswell's factual accuracy and narrative do not constitute the *Life*'s strength. Even though, as Paul Alkon has discussed, the apparent formlessness of Boswell's narrative sophisticatedly adapts time to the fictional life of Johnson that the book creates, it is the dramatic conversations and 'scenes' that are of greatest interest, and it is their place in the narrative that facilitates the presentation of Johnson's 'essence'. To a degree unmatched by any previous or subsequent biographer Boswell has made Johnson's character (as opposed to his life-in-time) the subject of the book. Therefore he did not have to adhere to strict factual accuracy. Rader remarks that Boswell 'gives not the whole of Johnson's words but the essence of them, preserving only the spirit and ... the effect of Johnson's talk and the atmosphere of the moment as listeners felt it' (28). From the detail and particulars of Johnson's life Boswell creates an image of Johnson that unifies the *Life* as a work of art, while lifting Johnson out of the constrictions of quotidian life and historical obscurity, thereby making him available to posterity as an object of moral emulation and admiration. This ideal conception of Boswell's biographical art is widely accepted, and underlies the readiness to credit the representational accuracy of Boswell's Johnson.

Behind it, however, lies a division between factual and fictional works which eliminates truth as a meaningful concept.

To see the art of the *Life* as self-contained, and opposed to a historical realm, cuts the ground from under the feet of the biographer. Boswellians commonly identify fact with truth and confine them to the historical and material world, where they are assumed to be separate from imagination and art. The fact that biography is a genre depicting the actual, historical life of a person, and that this naturally raises questions of truth and accuracy, is problematic for many Boswellians. Bogel and Dowling, for example, deal with the issue of truth by equating it with fact and then deconstructing the equation in order to prove that 'reality' and 'meaning' are merely textual. They argue that because the presence of the historical Johnson ('unmediated presence') is impossible in writing, therefore 'truth' is non-existent and Boswell's Johnson can only be a *mere* fiction, existing solely within its own terms. This emphasises the self-containment of the *Life* as a principle of coherence, removes the notion of accountability and evidence, and also diminishes the possibility of Boswell teaching us anything about Johnson. Waingrow says that 'Samuel Johnson will always be somebody's hypothesis' (1). But if Johnson is *only* the creation of Boswell's (or someone else's) text, then what the biographer teaches us *about* Johnson and, indeed, about life and art, is a meaningless question.

However, the mutually exclusive opposition between fiction and imagination on the one hand, and truth and history on the other – an idea shared even by such an implacable critic of Boswell as Donald Greene – echoes a tension and a duality in Boswell's thinking. It also responds to a contradiction in Boswell's conception of biography which goes to the heart of the *Life* but which, paradoxically, has contributed to its high estimation in this century.

Throughout the *Life*, but particularly in the 1791 and 1793 advertisements and in the opening pages of the text, Boswell claims merely to be transcribing fact when he is shaping complex images and making many artistic choices. The opening pages make two related points: (i) the *Life* will constitute a monument to the memory of Johnson – specifically, that Johnson 'will be seen as he really was', that by means of a 'scrupulous authenticity', the readers will be 'better acquainted with [Johnson], than even most of those were who actually knew him' (8, 22); and (ii) the *Life* will embalm Johnson in a kind of mausoleum (*Corr.* 96, 111–12, 146). The repeated assurances that the Johnson we are given is 'authentic' suggest Boswell's underplaying what might be seen as an inauthenticating artifice.

In one sense Boswell is acting no differently from eighteenth-century novelists, who repeatedly assure readers that the substance of their story is real and historical and that their account of experience was a faithful 'recording' of historical circumstances. Like Boswell, their imaginative and linguistic habits grew out of diary-keeping, an activity that proliferated in Protestant England, Scotland, and America in the late seventeenth and early eighteenth centuries. The tradition of autobiography and biography developed from the habits of observation and empirical recording that diaries (especially among puritans) made familiar. But for Boswell there is a problem in the relation between art and history not evident in Defoe, Richardson, or Fielding. He seems to half-believe that the rhetorical, metaphorical presence of Johnson in the *Life* is in fact real and immediate, and therefore historical. Although this blurring of fact and fiction might be a rhetorical ploy on Boswell's part as naive narrator to maximise the effectiveness of his details, the frequency with which he returns to the issue suggests that it masks a desire for *a priori* historical reality unambiguously and directly related to the biographer's artifice. It also suggests that Boswell understood that the issue involved personal and artistic difficulties.

Boswell's belief that his art will make Johnson more fully known than he was in life, *in the same way* as he was known in life, is paradoxical. It implies a concern to produce not just any image of Johnson, but one that Boswell believes is authentic and factual. It implies, therefore, something more than artistic choices; Boswell's self and self-definition are involved fundamentally. When Boswell creates images of Johnson as a being fully, vividly present in his physical and spiritual dimensions, and as a man troubled by melancholy and torn by moral awareness, triumphing over the evils, suffering, imperfections and temptations of this world in a grand affirmation of a Christian path, he tells us something about Johnson, but also about his own values, concerns, and sensibility. Since this is not the only or even the most obvious way of reading Johnson's life, especially if − contrary to Macaulay's opinion − we read Johnson's works with openness, Boswell's Johnson belongs not only to biography, but also to Boswellian *auto*biography, as modern scholarship has implicitly recognised for decades.

Fully acknowledging the autobiographical basis of the *Life of Johnson* means that any serious attempt to understand Johnson biographically or critically (or to understand Boswell for that matter) should not overlook the independence from Boswell of Johnson's position. To create a theoretical context, as many modern critics have, eliminating the importance of the difference between Johnson and Boswell, making Johnson no more than a self-contained, self-referential fiction in Boswell's art, is to deprive the biographical form of its leverage and power, and effectively to deprive Boswell of the meaning and substantiality that, as I demonstrate below, he seeks through his portrayal of Johnson. At the same time, Boswell's artistic appropriation of Johnson is not fully acknowledged by the biographer because it contravenes his belief in Johnson's autonomy, that he wants to transcribe.

Between these two entities in Boswell's text falls the shadow of the unacknowledged motives that govern many of his artistic choices and the tone of the *Life*. An important instance of this double consciousness, discussed in chapter 5 (pp. 85−97 below), is the discrepancy between the combative, conservative, moral Johnson presented in the conversations, and the independent insight into his mind that his works facilitate, but which Boswell either radically underplays or appropriates according to his own idea of Johnson. But Boswell's interpretation of Johnson is offered as true and historically independent. The implicit and explicit claim to authenticity, I suggest, assures Boswell of the past's (and his own) unassailability and independence. Bogel says that Boswell's claim for the status of his artistic image of Johnson 'is not really a critical assertion about the character of the historical order ... [but] an invest- ment of faith in the ability to break through the mediacy of one's own life, an ability that Johnson, in his moments of heroic presence, seems to demonstrate' ('Johnson Plain' 77). Below I demonstrate that Boswell's art and the particular image of Johnson that he constructs testify to the belief in the immediacy of life that Bogel mentions. But Boswell is an artist through and through, so that his claim is also to an independence that is fictional in that it accompanies a sense of potential dissolution and insubstantiality, a constant doubt for Boswell that the more he asserted or contrived its reality, the more likely it was to reveal itself as illusory and unable to sustain a *modus vivendi*, a self in action. This is the principle on which he constructs two endings for the *Life of Johnson* (see chapter 5, pp. 103 – 12 below), and that informs his perpetual desire to have Johnson's opinions and his own coincide, even when he documents their divergence. The divergence, how- ever, is crucial. Hence Boswell's inescapable effort and con- scientiousness to incarnate the image of Johnson he imagined. But this sometimes left him caught within the confines of his own self, unable, I will suggest, either to comprehend or to imagine the general nature of Johnson's writing and character.

Chapter 3

The structure of Boswell's experience and the *Life*

While it was once possible to consider Boswell as the writer of one popular book – the *Life of Johnson* – it has become clear that there are essential links between it and the Journals (1762–95), the *Account of Corsica* (1769), and the *Journal of a Tour to the Hebrides* (1785). In this section I suggest ways in which Boswell's biographical–artistic conception of, and his psychological relationship with, Johnson in the *Life* is rooted in and develops through these other works. Primarily I wish to indicate how Boswell's lifelong search for independence, self, and authority, as expressed in the Journals, furnishes metonymic paradigms for the essential psychological and narrative structure of the *Life*, and informs his dynamic relationship with Johnson at the heart of the *Life*.

Boswell's Journals and the representation of experience

Boswell's relation to his own experience never changes substantially. The young man's urgent search for assurance and for freedom on his first extended visit to London in 1762–3, recorded in *London Journal*, is as evident in his later Journals (such as *Boswell for the Defence*) as, indeed, it is in a transformed form in the *Life of Johnson*. Boswell's search for self is accompanied by a double consciousness, and predicates itself on a psychic paradox which determines that he is most afraid of what he needs most deeply.

The opening words of the *London Journal* suggest the different demands with which Boswell struggles throughout his journals: 'A man cannot know himself better than by attending to the feelings of his heart and to his external actions, from which he may with tolerable certainty judge "what manner of person he is"'; and 'knowing that I am to record my transactions will make me more careful to do well' (39). Boswell will know himself by knowing his feelings, yet his prose suggests a division between feelings and 'external actions'; it also indicates that the self-consciousness of transcribing his life will influence Boswell's actions – he will be careful to do well so that he can record it.

Boswell's interest in recording his life demonstrates a belief in his freedom to will himself into being. After a few days in London in 1762 he has 'discovered that we may be in some degree whatever character we choose. Besides, practice forms a man to anything' (*LJ* 47). Indeed, Boswell's manner of recording his own experience, making and unmaking it, and the momentary creation of his sense of self, tally with the postmodernist view that 'self' is not a reified thing, but an ideological and linguistic construct, a 'locus of discourses' (Nussbaum, 'Diary' 128–32). Yet Boswell is disturbed by the inability of his enabling fiction to provide him with substantial support for moral action and for personal identity. While his imagination transforms his particular experiences into the fiction of a continuous and coherent self, he is simultaneously unable to fully believe in his fiction, to find it equivalent to his idea or experience of reality. Boswell's writing is unable to sustain or create an integrity between the intellect and the feelings. This abiding interest in self responds to Hume's sceptical treatment of personal identity in *A Treatise of Human Nature* (1739–40), in which he drove a wedge between rational thinking about identity and the experience of perceiving one's own sensations (see Manning, 'Philosophical Melancholy'). Boswell was fascinated and worried for most of his life by Hume's sceptical treatment of knowledge and religious experience. How he uses Hume as a means of focusing on Johnson in the *Life* is dealt with more fully below (pp. 97–103). Generally, Boswell was disturbed by Hume's urbane argument that identity is constructed from moment to moment by the memory and imagination: 'when I enter most intimately into what I call *myself*, I always stumble on some particular perception or other, of heat or cold, light or shade, love or hatred, pain or pleasure. I can never catch *myself* at any time without a perception, and never can observe any thing but the perception' (*Treatise*, ed. L.A. Selby-Bigge (Oxford, 1978), 252). Boswell manifests this disturbance in a division between the style and the conviction of self in his writing, between his public and his private identities, and by the compulsive attempts to will into being a self and his relation to others and the world.

The following passage from the *London Journal* focuses all the above issues:

I was mentioning Erskine's character to Sir James Macdonald, a young man who has made a great figure at Eton school and the University of Oxford and is studying hard to fit himself for Parliament, being full of notions of the consequence of real life, and making a figure in the world, and all that. When he heard Erskine's sentiments (which, by the by, are much my own, and which I mentioned just to see what he would say), he was perfectly stunned. 'Why,' said he, 'he must not be a man. He is unfit to live in human society. He is not of the species.' I was really entertained. 'Ah!' thought I, 'little do you know of how small duration the pleasure is of making one of these great figures that now swell before your ambitious imagination.'

Yet I do think it is a happiness to have an object in view which one keenly follows. It gives a lively agitation to the mind which is very pleasurable. I am determined to have a degree of Erskine's indifference, to make me easy when things go cross; and a degree of Macdonald's eagerness for real life, to make me relish things when they go well ... The great art I have to study is to balance these two different ways of thinking properly. It is very difficult to be keen about a thing which in reality you do not regard, and consider as imaginary. But I fancy it may do, as a man is afraid of ghosts in the dark, although he is sure there are none; or pleased with beautiful exhibitions on the stage, although he knows they are not real. Although the Judgment may know that all is vanity, yet Passion may ardently pursue. Judgment and Passion are very different.   (78–9)

Boswell wants to construct a self based on his perception of Erskine and Macdonald and exemplifies the double consciousness characteristic of his journals. While Erskine and Macdonald hold different, desirable ideals, Boswell's difficulty is twofold: (i) he is unable to envisage and to represent a means of integrating these perspectives into a single way of thinking and way of being; he is unable to make them part of 'himself', and (ii) he has difficulty in believing, in any meaningful sense, in the qualities with which his fancy endows Erskine and Macdonald. Boswell is aware of how outside of his actual experience they remain: 'It is very difficult to be keen about a thing which in reality you do not regard, and consider as imaginary.' The difficulty of wanting and not wanting to be keen about a thing arises from Boswell's propensity to see his experience as fictional – the metaphor is of 'beautiful exhibitions on a stage' – so that he becomes a spectator at his own play, always observing but never quite doing. Yet Boswell will not relinquish the imagined control that comes with observing, as opposed to the vulnerability of participation in experience. To employ a metaphor from film, he wishes to be both director and actor at once. While Judgement and Passion (as he conceives them) seem not to go together, he nonetheless believes that a 'proper' character *would* necessarily reconcile them. He is unable to accept that people generally 'reconcile' such large phenomena imperfectly.

Boswell's double consciousness both causes and stems from a wilful commitment to a perfection that can never be realised, and this is mirrored in the style of the above passage. The prose has the ease and intonation of the spoken voice, but the structural effort at balancing and modelling the thought and feeling ('The great art I have to study is to balance these two different ways of thinking properly') constantly break down and dissipate: 'It is very difficult to be keen about a thing which in reality you do not regard, and consider as imaginary.' The syntax moving back upon itself suggests an honesty, as if Boswell's thought is finding a more firmly realised, less imaginary level. But nothing solid materialises, for the one thought annihilates the other, leaving emptiness and inconsequentiality, and the prose suddenly moves off to another fantasy – 'But I fancy it may do, as a man is afraid of ghosts ...' Commitment to perfection keeps Boswell's fancy separate from his reasoning, and his reasoning separate from his feelings, while a *feeling* of connectedness and stability is what he seeks in the passage quoted and in much of his journal prose. While Boswell intellectually believes that a person can choose his or her character, he discovers, in practice, that this means being nobody. But his thinking cannot absorb and incorporate that knowledge on the level of self; it remains split off and susceptible to the imagination, but potentially confusing and so dangerous to the feelings. Boswell's language is either in excess of his feelings, or inadequate to them; his language is unable to record experience without generating a consciousness in excess of the self, beyond the present. This discrepancy is one of the ways of describing Boswell's melancholy. 'Melancholy is the refuge of the articulate self in the unsayable' (Manning, 'Philosophical Melancholy' 16).

Though Boswell's fictionalising is celebrated by modern critics as evidence of a postmodernist sensibility, for Boswell it entails suffering. In the space that opens up between thought and action arise Boswell's contradictory desires, one of the marks of his openness and of his confusion — to be ordinary and to be a man of genius, to be a rebellious gangster like Macheath in the *Beggar's Opera* (to whom he often compared himself) and to be a respectable Scottish laird like his father, to be pious and orderly in his domestic behaviour and to be a libertine. Boswell's habitual melancholy occurs in between these entities — the irreconcilability of these extremes makes for melancholy. In his journals he commonly tackles melancholy by escaping from it through role-playing, pantomime, and fantasy of one kind or another. But these alternatives retain melancholy as a primary datum of consciousness, ironically fixing in that which his writing attempts to eliminate. Consequently, no part of Boswell's experience has the independence that comes from resistance to the given; hence it lacks a sense of the real, and becomes instead a part of his subjective sensations and psychology. One of the reasons Boswell enjoys Johnson's company so much is because the emptiness he feels when thinking about his own life is filled by Johnson's presence. In the *Life* Boswell makes a great deal of Johnson's melancholy and his courage in handling it. Johnson's 'presence' is not merely personal and historical, but integral to a style of writing that builds into itself a recognition and acceptance of the facts, limits, and changes of life independent of the will or the imagination, in ways that contrast strikingly with Boswell's prose.

The following passage from *Rambler* 43, against the doctrine of innate ideas, might have been written as a gloss on Boswell's psychological and emotional struggles:

As every step in the progression of existence changes our position with respect to the things about us, so as to lay us open to new assaults and particular dangers, and subjects us to inconveniences from which any other situation is exempt; as a publick or a private life, youth or age, wealth and poverty, have all some evil closely adherent, which cannot wholly be escaped but by quitting the state to which it is annexed, and submitting to the incumbrances of some other condition; so it cannot be denied that every difference in the structure of the mind has its advantages and its wants; and that failures and defects, being inseparable from humanity, however the powers of the understanding be extended or contracted, there will on one side or the other always be an avenue to error or miscarriage. (*Rambler*, ed. W.J. Bate and A. Strauss, 3 vols. (Yale, 1968), I, 232–3)

This passage is about the difficulties and errors endemic in any undertaking or any form of being, but it feels to the reader like a positive affirmation of the mind's capacities and life's fruitfulness. Unlike Boswell's treatment of Erskine and Macdonald, where the idealisation of the two men is mutually exclusive and generates melancholy, Johnson perceives limits not as a mark of failed imagination, but as part of our nature, and thus constituting the field of activity. The individual is neither all active nor all passive within that field; limits are what we find as existing beyond us, yet as an intimate part of who we are, in the process of trying to transcend limits. Johnson's recognition that we usually see more than we can do, that our consciousness exceeds our action – 'the mind of man is never satisfied with the objects immediately before it, but is always breaking away from the present moment ... we forget the proper use of the time now in our power' (*Rambler* 2, I, 9) – discovers our boundaries *in* our inability to limit ourselves. Johnson turns Boswell's oppositions (Erskine/ Macdonald, Judgement/Passion, even, later, Johnson/Hume) into deeper, subtler perceptions of states of mind within one individual, and establishes connections between the levels of experience within the syntax. The quotation from *Rambler* 43 is one sentence, constituted by several subordinate clauses, each connecting the idea of change with a different 'danger', 'inconvenience', and 'evil' that can only be avoided by further change. But as the clauses unfold one 'evil' after another, it becomes clear that no change can entirely escape these eventualities. Just as that situation is accepted ('submitting to the incumbrances of some other condition'), so the prose turns upward and connects 'advantages' with the same 'evils'. The apparent contradiction is part of the meaning of Johnson's thought and it is integral to the structure of the prose; contradiction is avoided by the way the single sentence incorporates within itself the differences. The syntactical flexibility enacts what the passage calls the 'powers of understanding'. As the syntax encounters and then encompasses the idea of circumstantial and human differences, so it makes them 'part of humanity', and the structure of the sentence comes to feel inseparable from the structure of the way things are.

The structure of Johnson's passage recognises that the complexity of experience is not easily, straightforwardly encoded in writing. The limits of which Johnson writes are also the limits of his medium and of the mind working in it. This is transmitted to Johnson's sense of self. Unlike Boswell's use of Erskine and Macdonald, Johnson's prose reveals no firm idea of himself, but by feeling the 'incumbrances' of each situation as part of the 'outside' as well as part of the inside of his own mind, he opens his experience, and suggests a sustaining self. The feeling then is more spacious, open, and balanced than Boswell's. This is a self constituted by an integration of feeling and thinking, and it is expressed in writing even while the passage recognises the almost inveterate discrepancy between language and living.

Boswell has a different attitude to language; words are equated with things, so that writing-a-self is taken for having-a-self. However, sometimes the possibility that language might simply and directly correspond to reality threatens Boswell, as when he wonders whether the biblical language of damnation may be literal: 'I ventured to ask him [Johnson] whether, although the words of some texts of Scripture seemed strong in support of the dreadful doctrine of an eternity of punishment, we might not hope that the denunciation was figurative, and would not literally be executed' (*Life* 875). Both the literal, truth aspect of writing as well as its fictional possibilities can fail to satisfy, and Boswell's feelings are often also at odds with the fiction of self he carefully builds up.

Boswellians have accepted for decades that Boswell employs his fictionalising as part of a psychological–emotional search for figures from whom he could experience authority and nurturing. As Julia Kristeva suggests, the discrepant relationship between fiction and melancholy in Boswell's experience indicates an irrevocable, sometimes desperate separation from the mother, 'a loss that causes him to try to find her again, along with other objects of love, first in the imagination, then in words' (*Black Sun* (New York, 1989), 6). Seeking objects of love through words, I suggest, is an activity that Boswell directs not only at women but also at men, particularly Johnson (though at various times he also treated Dalrymple, Paoli, Rousseau, and Voltaire as such objects of love). This book demonstrates how Boswell's recreation of Johnson through art in the *Life of Johnson* enacts a primary experience of self-annihilation and self-affirmation; in Kristeva's words, 'the supporting father of such a symbolic triumph [over sadness, such as the *Life* is] is not the oedipal father but truly that "imaginary father", "father in individual prehistory" according to Freud, who guarantees primary identification' (23).

The father (Alexander Boswell, Lord Auchinleck) who gave Boswell so much trouble was a well-intentioned but unsympathetic and unimaginative man; but the internalised, symbolic father constructed by Boswell's needs and imagination was infinitely more fierce and unrelenting than the real man. By 1762–3, when Boswell was in London, his father was a Lord of Session (1754) and Lord of Justiciary (1755), and represented the respectability and power of the Scottish legal establishment. He was an old-fashioned patriotic Scottish Whig in the pre-union (1707) tradition, and a member of the Presbyterian Church of Scotland. In the sketch of his early life, written for Rousseau, Boswell remarks on the rigidity of the Presbyterian church, how his father had impressed upon him a respect for the truth, and how his mother had inculcated piety by the terrors of eternal punishment and the uncertainty of salvation (Pottle, *Earlier Years* 1–6). Boswell was temperamentally antithetical to his father, yet at the same time loved and admired him and wanted to please him. But while Boswell wanted to become an officer in the Guards – mainly as a means of staying in London and having a good time – his father wanted him to follow in the family tradition and to become an advocate. Boswell's unsteadiness as a young man, and the reports of his wildness in London that reached Auchinleck in 1762–3, prompted Alexander to give his son an ultimatum. The letter (printed in *LJ* 337–42) he wrote to Boswell on 30 May 1763 gives one a powerful sense of the psychological and political difficulties he represented for Boswell, and which Boswell carried with him all his life.

The destructiveness of Alexander's letter lies in the psychic and emotional double bind his contradictory demands and evasions generate in a receptive Boswell. These are expressed in three related ways. The father first affirms his right to authority over Boswell, then denies asserting it or wishing to assert it, and then disclaims having any after all. Boswell is next represented as 'bound' by the 'laws of God, nature, gratitude, and interest' to make his parents happy, but instead he brings upon them 'distresses and shame' (339–40, 342). Of particular distress to his father are Boswell's 'mimicry, journals, and publications' (342) – essentially Boswellian activities with which he occupied himself throughout his life. Finally Boswell is placed in a double bind: his father threatens him with disinheritance, in such a way as to exhibit his power, while presenting his action as being reluctantly arrived at, and, implicitly, Boswell's responsibility:

even I, who am your father and who, while you trod the paths of virtue and discretion was bound up in you and carried on all my projects with a view to you in whom I flattered myself to find a representative worthy of this respectable family – I say, even I by your strange conduct had come to the resolution of selling all off, from the principle that it is better to snuff a candle out than leave it to stink in a socket. (341)

The threat not only reasserts the primacy of the family dynasty and its respectability, but Alexander's metaphor equates Boswell's very existence with the continuance of the family, and reinforces the sense of the fragility and worthlessness of Boswell's life independent of the father's schema. Such psychological brutality ('snuff a candle ... stink in a socket') would perhaps threaten existentially even one with a stronger sense of self than Boswell. Not only does the father have no understanding of the son's needs – 'What you mean by becoming independent I am at a loss to conceive' (340) – but the very language in which he makes what he takes to be rational demands in fact displaces his feelings on to Boswell, and implicitly makes Boswell responsible (that is, guilty) for them: 'It is in your power to make us all happy and yourself too' (342). It is this assertion of a political and personal power, in a rhetoric which denies its existence, for the purposes of generating moral, intellectual, and emotional good for Boswell (and *not* for the explicit purpose of hurting him), which inculcates the threatening psychological vertigo he exemplifies so often in the *London Journal* and, in a different fashion, in the *Life*.

The threat his father poses is especially clear in Boswell's evasiveness on the particular issue. Not only does Boswell reiterate, in response to the letter, that his father is 'one of the best men in the world', but he writes to Sir David Dalrymple denying all anxiety associated with disinheritance: 'it is not from fear of being disinherited (which he threatens) that I am anxious. I am thoughtless enough not to mind that. But my affection for him makes me very unhappy at the thoughts of offending him' (*LJ* 274, 276). That Boswell's affection for his father is sincere is entirely believable; what makes it anxious and unhappy, of course, is that it cannot trust the safety of the world in which it finds itself. So the transparent coolness of Boswell's statement about disinheritance also reveals great unacknowledged concern.

Boswell's response, then, to his father's threat and demand that he, Boswell, should study law in Holland is to capitulate, and then to persuade himself that this has discharged his duty to make his father happy. However, the price for such psychological self-deception is an emotional self-alienation, splitting off the feelings from the reality of events: 'I felt a great degree of satisfaction at thinking that my father would now be happy, and all things go well, and that I might indulge whim with a higher relish' (277). The father's abuse of power seems only to tempt Boswell to take deeper refuge from responsibility in 'whim'. In other words, the particular manner of Boswell's self-representation in the Journals, and the psychological and literary characteristics of his melancholy discussed above, constitute one way of dealing with the existential threat and the anxiety of affection associated with his father. Below I suggest that Boswell's manner of dealing with these difficulties in the *Life of Johnson* − trying, for example, to obtain the love and independence not offered by his father − incorporates and inverts some of the very methods used by his father.

Those methods are less evident in Boswell's relation to Johnson in the *London Journal* than they are in the *Life*. When Boswell tells Johnson his story in the *London Journal*, Johnson does two things the father never does, and which Boswell craves. He says, ' "Give me your hand. I have taken a liking to you." ' And then he 'confirmed me [Boswell] in my belief, by showing the force of testimony, and how little we could know of final causes; so that the objections of why was it so? or why was it not so? can avail little' (283). In other words, Johnson accepts Boswell for the person he is, and invites him to release his anxiety at the inability to answer all the religious and moral questions which trouble Boswell throughout his life, but which also represent a general human inability to comprehend final causes. Johnson is talking about a fundamental aspect of Boswell's melancholy, what might be called the unreconstructed sceptical or Humean side of Boswell's life − a desperate doubt of experience underlying the strong need for intellectual certainty and emotional security. At the same time, neither the assurances offered by such pseudo-mentors as Rousseau or Dalrymple, nor the relief Boswell felt in Johnson's presence, are quite able to satisfy him psychologically and emotionally.

The need for autonomy and for relatedness is a central challenge in Boswell's life and writing. Boswell's first major parting from Johnson, in August 1763 when he left England for study in Holland and the Grand Tour, recorded in both the *London Journal* and the *Life*, depicts a painful experience, a pain apparently in excess of the facts of the situation:

> [Johnson] said, 'There are few people whom I take so much to as you'; and when I [Boswell] talked of leaving England, he said (with an affection that almost made me cry), 'My dear Boswell! I should be very unhappy at parting, did I think we were not to meet again.'
>
> (*LJ* 321)

It is Johnson who is comfortable enough here to express his feeling – his affection and sadness – at parting from Boswell, but this is Boswell's prose; it is he who almost (but not quite) cries, and who records the situation so simply and movingly. The same scene in the *Life* (318) twenty-eight years later eliminates the reference to tears (which makes the passage from the *London Journal* poignant and human), and instead concerns itself with defending Boswell against a hypothetical charge of vanity: 'I cannot too often remind my readers, that although such instances of his kindness are doubtless very flattering to me, yet I hope my recording them will be ascribed to a better motive than vanity' (318). The substitution is strange particularly in the light of the natural pride he feels when Johnson decides to see him off at Harwich (327), and the tenderness he records at the moment of their parting in Harwich (334). The change from the *London Journal* to the *Life* specified above suggests how instrumental (in *both* versions) the tears were for Boswell in holding on to Johnson. The *London Journal*, I suggest, documents how difficult it was for Boswell to let go of Johnson, and the *Life* how difficult it was to hold on to him.

Boswell's sexuality and the representation of Johnson

The empowerment Boswell seeks in Johnson's company, and that he documents in the Journals and the *Life*, he also seeks in sex. In this section I want briefly to suggest how Boswell's sexual politics forms a paradigm for his fictional, created relationship with Johnson in the *Life*. In the *London Journal* sex is prominent in Boswell's self-definition. Many have recognised that in his relation to women Boswell needs to feel superior for psychological and political reasons. Seduction and sexual performance are precursors of the grandiose self-image Boswell seeks in his exploits. But while Boswell's sexual activity and alcoholism became a means of dealing with (or, in fact, not really dealing with) unintegrated psychological and emotional needs (especially after 1774), the *London Journal* reveals that his real needs are for love and acceptance, and that they are inversely but directly related to his habitual manipulation and fantasisation. Being an object of abusive paternal power, Boswell psychically attempts to undo its effects by imitating its methods, but as with his general method of writing-the-self discussed above, the seductive relation he cultivates towards women, powerful men (such as the Duke of Northumberland, Rousseau, Voltaire, and notably Johnson), and society itself actually undercuts his real purpose even while it achieves the ostensible object of his desire.

Most obviously Boswell maintains his imprisonment within this psychic double bind by indulging in sexual activity with whores, people for whom he has no respect and affection, so that sex brings relief but also self-disgust and genuflexion: 'I ... took the first whore I met ... I never asked her name. When it was done, she slunk off. I had a low opinion of this gross practice and resolved to do it no more ... I could not but despise myself for being so closely united with such a low wretch' (231, 256). Sex of this kind is, apparently, fated to exclude pleasure, and to reinforce the supposition of Boswell's own unworthiness. This is one failure of Boswell's to extirpate the effects of the Calvinist theology he inherited from his family and culture – a 'failure' that encourages him to continue seeing himself as a worthless, unredeemed victim of his own appetites and nature.

Even more desirable and pleasurable sexual connections, such as the affairs with Louisa, Lady Caroline Judd, and Belle de Zuylen, occasioned anxieties. Louisa was the stage name of Mrs Anne Lewis, a small-time actress Boswell had known slightly in Edinburgh, and who was twenty-four years old in January 1763 when their London liaison began (Pottle, *Earlier Years* 98). In this affair (recounted in the *London Journal*) the studied artifice of Boswell's autoerotic language is evasive and emotionally disconnected from events in much the way his prose was shown to work when writing about Erskine and Macdonald. Sexual intercourse is described in grandiose, romantic, euphemistic language suggestive of the cynicism of the libertines of Restoration drama (such as Sir John Brute, in Vanbrugh's *Provok'd Wife*, with whom Boswell associates himself [227]). In seducing Louisa, Boswell is aware of playing an elaborate game with its own romantic rhetoric, thereby distancing events, as if they were happening on a stage, and Boswell a spectator, only an imaginative participant (e.g. 94–5, 117). Impotence – even the *appearance* of impotence – troubles Boswell; but his response to this is to represent his actions as being divorced from his bodily experience. While this might permit Boswell to entertain himself with his own drama, it only intensifies the anxiety associated with selfhood and performance, and makes the whole experience narcissistic because devoid of bodily experience, and disconnected from nature. This is another form of melancholy.

Two parts of the relationship with Louisa are worth looking at in detail: the symbolic function of money, and Boswell's attitude to the venereal disease he contracts. Both issues have resonant connections with the body, both as textual metaphor and, immediately connected to that, as an experience in Boswell's life. These issues underlie Boswell's attitude to Johnson's literal, bodily presence, and to his symbolic presence in the *Life*.

When giving money to Louisa at the beginning of their liaison (*LJ* 96–8, 20 December 1762), Boswell is unsure whether her financial need is a means of tricking him, or an innocent appeal to his 'generosity and regard for her'. He lends her two guineas, but offers her up to ten, should she need it; he then assures himself that 'ten guineas was but a moderate expense for women during the winter', and, ironically (as it turns out), 'it cost me as much to be cured of what I contracted from a whore' (97). Although he does not wish to be too demanding of her affections on this occasion, 'lest it should look like demanding goods for my money', they make a date for the future and Boswell leaves 'highly pleased with the thoughts of the affair being settled' (97, 98). In fact, Boswell has paid his money in anticipation of future favours.

Between 20 December and 12 January 1763, when they finally have a night of lovemaking, Boswell is troubled by the 'anxiety of serious love' (100), by a melancholy related to the uncertainty of how he will perform sexually, and by whether he might appear to her to be impotent during the *intervening* period (117, 126). The contortions he goes through to impress the woman before 12 January, and to convince himself of his enjoyment, reveal that Boswell's relation to Louisa is part of a grandiose but sad exercise in creating a potent image of himself through sexual prowess and monetary expenditure. Later it becomes clear that for Boswell money is equated with power, and that it eliminates (or is expected to eliminate) vulnerability, the possibility of rejection, and therefore of vacancy and melancholy. The elaborate courting game that the couple is dramatised as playing is a socially acceptable means of facilitating sex, but for Boswell it also psychologically eliminates the woman as independent Other. She becomes part of the fictional world of the *London Journal*, and therefore a plank in the edifice of self-construction the Journal undertakes.

When Boswell hears on 19 January that he is infected with a venereal disease, the edifice receives a profound shaking. His immediate feeling is a fear of the 'poisonous infection raging in my veins' – 'having the distemper thrown into my blood terrified me exceedingly'; but this is quickly transformed into 'anxiety and vexation boiling in my breast' (155, 156).

The anxiety, it seems, stems from three parts of Boswell's experience: (i) the feeling of victimisation — this was something he did not bargain for, and could not foresee (even though he had been infected before); (ii) the sense of impotence at being unable to control the situation (he strains to understand, intellectually, the stark contrast between the beauty and the 'corruption' of the woman); and (iii) the knowledge that his body has a life of its own independent of his mind and its image-making capacities. It is significant that the physical discomfort and the anxiety he feels are immediately understood as Louisa's (not his own) 'corruption'.

The psychological projection involved in the scenario he creates for himself continues in Boswell's account of actually confronting Louisa (on the 20th, 158–60) and in his letter requesting repayment of the money (174–5). In the Journal Boswell creates a dialogue form to dramatise his feelings. Both 'Louisa' and 'Boswell' himself are fictionalised personae performing a routine apparently designed to establish Boswell's power over her and over his feelings of helplessness. The dialogue concludes by making her indebted to him for his discretion and 'honour', and then by congratulating Boswell on his 'manly composure' and 'polite dignity' (160). But the self-aggrandising fantasy in this dialogue cannot eliminate the real source of the hurt and the anger: 'I am afraid that you don't love me so well, nor have not such a regard for me, as I thought you had' (159). However, Boswell cannot directly acknowledge this since it would necessitate a recognition and an acceptance of his helplessness, and his naturalness rooted in the reality of his bodily experience. So he resorts to a caricatured Othello-like passion: 'Cunning jade', 'What the devil does the confounded jilt mean by being hurt in her circumstances? This is the grossest cunning' (159, 160).

The ostensible purpose of Boswell's letter to Louisa is to request his money, but its unacknowledged emotional purpose is to punish her who 'deserved to suffer for her depravity': 'If you are not rendered callous by a long course of disguised wickedness, I should think the consideration of your deceit and baseness, your corruption both of body and mind, would be a very severe punishment' (175). While this letter claims intellectual and moral superiority for Boswell, the punishment he envisages for Louisa ('corruption of both body and mind') is Boswell's unconscious projection. Boswell is at present the one whose body might be said to be 'corrupted', and who therefore feels mentally corrupted. Deceitful and base are how her behaviour appears to a man whose *ideas* (of her and of himself) have proved to be unfounded. In fancy he sought purity and the ideal; corruption of body and mind is how purity and the ideal look to the disembodied fancy when real experiences take their toll.

The same confusion of feelings pertains to Boswell's attitude to money as to venereal disease. He reflects that the mention of money might not be polite in a letter to a person even of Louisa's standing. But because in his experience money has a self-potentiating power, therefore 'pecuniary punishment will give [her] most pain' (175). But when she returns the money (187), without any word attached, Boswell is confused. Her action finally ends the relationship; but Boswell's 'tender heart relented', and he thinks of sending the money back as a token of *his* 'atonement'. But his friend Dempster convinces him that Louisa's action is 'just a piece of deep artifice', so Boswell consoles himself with being two guineas better off. Since money is a metaphor for power, possession, and autonomy in Boswell's thinking – attempting to take the place of love, acceptance, and connectedness – it atones for his semi-conscious feelings of self-disgust and worthlessness.

In fact, Boswell's escapade with Louisa, as dramatised in the *London Journal*, is a form of secular atonement for the demands of an internalised Calvinist theology that takes human needs and nature as evidence of the absence of grace in life (Manning, *Puritan–Provincial Vision* 8–9). Boswell's search for self and authority in the Louisa episode, as elsewhere, enacts what Susan Manning says about Puritan writing in general, that it 'lacks the means to express not merely provisionality but acquiescence: the giving up of self to God obtains – in the prose – no release through spirituality or self-forgetfulness' (12). But Boswell does not know what to do with the discrepancy that arises between the language of his journal and his experience of loss and corruption. Ironically, Boswell's manner of attaining the selfhood he cherishes − of bringing language and object together − takes a form of coercion and control such as he experiences at the hands of his father: Louisa is always a fictionalised and therefore completely assimilated object in his world. Hence his victimised feelings *while* expending great energy in controlling and manipulating the desired outcome. This activity is narcissistic because energy is invested in an image, an idea of self that evades the reality of bodily experiences whose incorporation is necessary for a true, fundamental sense of self capable of being *in* the world. Boswell's response to his disease indicates how psychologically difficult it is for him to know and accept his own experience, and the limits of the will in the face of life's unpredictability.

The above consideration of the seduction of Louisa makes it possible to make some propositions about the significance of the body in Boswell's writing. The body is the psychological and emotional locus of all Boswell's writing, including the *Life of Johnson*. It operates metaphorically, as it does in the interest in 'writing the body' espoused by such French feminists as Julia Kristeva and Hélène Cixous, and in the particular application of these theories to the *Life* by Donna Heiland and William Dowling. But Boswell's interest in the body is also ontological and phenomenological; it involves his immediate experience of himself and of the world, as well as how these two areas are created, fictionalised and understood in his writing. In the search for the Other, via his relationship with Louisa, Boswell appropriates the woman so that her independent otherness becomes an artistic reflection of his own feared, 'corrupted', unaccepted, yet very real body. A similar process vis-à-vis Johnson takes place in the elaborate artistic construction of the image of 'Samuel Johnson' Boswell offers in the *Life of Johnson*.

Boswell habitually appropriates difference in his relationship with others and the wider world. Unwanted separation, of course, threatens psychic death. It is significant that Boswell's failure to win acquittal of John Reid for sheep-stealing, in

1774, represents a great psychological defeat for him (he documents the episode at length in *Boswell for the Defence*). Boswell identified strongly with his client, John Reid; in relation to the Edinburgh legal establishment, both Boswell and Reid are outsiders. Patricia Spacks notes that the defeat (confirmed by Lord Auchinleck, the judge who condemned Reid to death) represented for Boswell a diminishment of his own prestige and legal and linguistic capacities, and that it also brought him face to face with the reality of death and his own contingency, from which some part of him did not recover (273–4).

It is in Johnson's presence that Boswell found contingency and limits mysteriously transformed into strengths. This is one of the reasons why Johnson's physicality, his body, is so important in the imaginative world of the *Life*. Johnson's physical particularities are expressive of his moral nature, and integral to the vision Boswell has of him. Critics have recognised that Johnson's body is the numinous, focal, 'recollected' object of the *Life*. The separation between Boswell and Johnson represented by death – an image of historical, cultural, psychic distance – is what Boswell's biographical method aims to overcome through memory. Metaphorically memory is the re-membering, the putting back together of Johnson's bodily presence disintegrated by death. The rhetoric of seduction of the journals is replayed in the *Life* most clearly in Boswell's manipulative manner, in the ways he gets Johnson to speak about or be in the places he wants. The visit to the former home of the poet Edward Young, or the episode in which Boswell contrives for Johnson to dine with John Wilkes, the radical libertine, against Johnson's previously expressed principles, are only two occasions on which Boswell 'seduces' Johnson (the Wilkes episode is discussed more fully below). Almost like a rival lover, Boswell prided himself on being able to get Johnson to perform in a manner unmatched by Mrs Thrale, the main challenge to Boswell's claim to intimacy with Johnson, and hence to possessing his memory, symbolically to possessing his remains, his body.

Hence the metaphoric resonance of Boswell's use of burial terms to describe the object and the method of his art:

I tell every body it [the *Life*] will be an Egyptian Pyramid in which
there will be a compleat mummy of Johnson that Literary Monarch.
(Letter to Anna Seward, 1785; *Corr.* 96)

it is my design in writing the Life of that Great and Good Man, to
put as it were into a Mausoleum all the precious remains that I can
gather.
(Letter to Joseph Walker, 1785; *Corr.* 111–12)

The comparison of the biography to a mausoleum and the
image of Johnson to a mummy suggest the ontological significance of the historical and the fictionalised Johnson. It also
raises the question of Boswell's relation to and freedom from
Johnson's 'body'. This relationship is essential since it determines the content, the structure, and the tone of the *Life* – in
short, its status as a work of art, and therefore as a biography.

Boswell's biographical narrative: the *Tour* and *Corsica*

Boswell's biographical works are *An Account of Corsica,
The Journal of a Tour to that Island; and Memoirs of Pascal
Paoli* (Glasgow, 1768), *The Journal of a Tour to the Hebrides
with Samuel Johnson, LL.D.* (London, 1785), and *The Life
of Samuel Johnson, LL.D.* (London, 1791). In their own way
each of these works invokes 'authenticity' as a moral touchstone and as a structuring principle. Of the presentation of the
character of Paoli, Boswell says in the Preface to *Corsica*: 'as
I have related his remarkable sayings, I declare upon honour,
that I have neither added nor diminished ... I know with how
much pleasure we read what is perfectly authentick' (xiii).
The Dedication (to Edmund Malone) of the *Tour* echoes this
assertion: 'In every narrative, whether historical or biographical,
authenticity is of the utmost consequence' (155). However,
in the *Life* authenticity does not imply a simple documentary
reliance on fact to the exclusion of conscious imaginative
artifice, though Boswell's conception of authenticity does
change between the 1760s and 1790s.

To trace this change is to recognise a shift in Boswell's conception of memory from a basic Baconian and Humean notion
– memory as the empirical manifestation of the structural

principle of personal and scientific identity and historical continuity − to a more pseudo-transcendental conception to be found in romantic idealism (in Coleridge's aesthetics, for example). It is also to recognise the change in Boswell's conception of history from the political and moral exemplary conception of Clarendon, Bolingbroke, and (behind them) Plutarch, to a more overtly redemptive, ideal, and universal notion of history espoused by such German historiographers as Schiller and Wilhelm von Humboldt. The focal point of these large changes in style and sensibility is Boswell's conception and presentation of the character of his protagonist, and his particular relation to that figure in the work. While the character of Paoli is part of a larger political purpose in *Corsica* of advocating the liberty of the Corsicans, and while the Johnson of the *Tour* is presented in a relatively static manner designed to complement the larger exercise in cultural anthropology, the *Life* is more flexible, diverse, inward, and personal in its conception of Johnson's character, and it employs a more dramatic presentation of character than either of the earlier works.

The biographical presentation of Pascal Paoli in *Corsica* is shaped by the general political purpose of the work. Boswell visited Corsica on the encouragement of Rousseau who had foreshadowed the political independence of the Corsicans along the lines propounded in the *Social Contract* (1762), and who had just received an invitation to draft a constitution for the emerging nation. Corsican politics constituted a long history of struggle to establish a national identity and independence from various oppressors, and young Boswell's political idealism was perhaps infused with a sympathy for the failed Jacobite uprisings of 1745−6 and the connection of those uprisings with a romantic vision of a new independence and history for Scotland. In the 1760s France was in the process of acquiring the island from Genoa, the British having effectively abandoned the Corsicans to their fate after the peace of Aix-la-Chapelle (1748). In 1755 Paoli (1725−1807) returned from exile to become general, establishing a peace among warring factions and beginning to create a civilised social structure. Paoli saw Boswell's visit (11 October to 20 November 1765) as an opportunity to use the young man as an unofficial diplomat to gain British support for Corsican independence (Curley 5 and *passim*).

Boswell undertook the impossible task with zest and conscientiousness, and crafted his work so as to present the most flattering and encouraging view of Corsica and its general to his readership (Siebenschuh, *Form and Purpose* chapter 2, and Curley). Liberty is the central concern of *Corsica* around which all issues revolve, and which draw together Boswell's interest in personal and public modes of maturation: 'Liberty is so natural, and so dear to mankind, whether as individuals, or as members of society, that it is indispensibly necessary to our happiness' (1). In the bulk of the book Boswell surveys the island's geography and natural history, its political, revolutionary history, and its government and culture, so as to suggest that they are all natural and powerful expressions of the principle of liberty openly invoked in the Introduction. They complement the more biographical (and autobiographical) 'Journal and Memoirs of Paoli', at the centre of which stands Boswell's portrait of Paoli, an ideal, heroic embodiment of the political and cultural ideals expressed throughout the work. Siebenschuh remarks of the structure of the whole work, that the *Account* is a piece of propaganda originally linked to the *Tour* and *Memoirs* whose aim was 'to present Paoli as both a romantic and heroic extension of the virtues of his people and yet a leader ... with whom a country like Britain could negotiate formally' (14). And where the *Account of Corsica* dramatises Liberty in historiographical terms, the *Tour to Corsica* and *Memoirs* develop the Plutarchian biographical form: virtue and liberty realised in personal terms. In the narrative depiction of Paoli, Boswell humanises the Plutarchian ideal (Brodwin 80).

Integral to that process of humanising is Boswell's emphasis on the exemplary nature and practical effect of Paoli's character. Boswell makes Paoli's demeanour express what his character embodies: 'His carriage and deportment prejudiced them in his favour, and his superior judgment, and patriotick spirit,

displayed with all the force of eloquence, charmed their under-
standings. All this, heightened with condescension, affability
and modesty, entirely won their hearts' (127). In the process
of exemplifying the Plutarchian idea that 'moral beauty or
virtue can transform the nature of the "soul" and move the
Will ... to realize itself in a world of personal and political
action' (Brodwin 74), Boswell finds an eminent, authoritative
man of the world with whom he can continue the process of
education conducted on the Grand Tour (with Earl Marischal,
Voltaire, Rousseau, Wilkes) and, before that, with Johnson
and others in London. He says of Paoli:

His notions of morality are high and refined, such as becomes the
Father of a nation ... He told me that his father had brought him
up with great strictness, and that he had very seldom deviated from
the paths of virtue. That this was not from a defect of feeling or
passion, but that his mind being filled with important objects, his
passions were employed in more noble pursuits than those of licentious
pleasure.   (302–3)

The very act of being with and writing about Paoli is education-
al for Boswell, and furthers a cause morally and imaginatively
attractive to him.

Paoli is presented as fully formed, without any complex
psychological subtleties or personal details characteristic of
Boswell's later biographical portraits. Paoli exemplifies the
highest political and moral virtues, yet he exists in a Classical,
ideal world, beyond the dramatic immediacy of Johnson's
life as represented in the *Life*. This is perhaps an aspect of
Boswell's artistic purpose; he may have used a different method
in portraying Paoli after the general had been exiled in London
(June 1769) and he and Boswell became closer friends. In the
presentation of Paoli in *Corsica*, however, there is a direct
and simple relation between being and action – what Paoli
is he exhibits – that is not typical of either of the portraits
of Johnson.

Boswell uses similar monumental imagery to describe the
effect of Paoli and Johnson on himself – when particularly
impressed by Paoli's sayings, he notes: 'This uttered with the
fine open Italian pronunciation, and the graceful dignity of

his manner, was very noble. I wished to have a statue of him taken at that moment' (320–1). But Johnson's character is more complex morally; his is an inner fallen Christian world, where the shadow constantly falls between the thought and the action, and where Johnson's heroism manifests itself in dealing with that moral fissure in humankind's experience and in overcoming it with grandeur.

The *Tour*, however, is like *Corsica* in isolating the subject from other phenomena with which he is nominally in relation. In the *Tour*, a work based on the journals Boswell kept during his journey with Johnson through the Scottish Highlands and Hebrides from 14 August to 11 November 1773, Johnson's character is already fully formed, and the emphasis falls on Johnson's interaction with Scottish culture, history, and land-scape. In comparison to the *Life*, the Johnson of the *Tour* is relatively static, identified by bold traits, and embodies English culture in a Scottish setting. By 1773, Boswell had known Johnson for eleven years, and their close relationship was already well established. Boswell already had a complex sense of his English friend, as the opening portrait of Johnson testifies. The Scottish tour, however, is the longest continuous period of time that Johnson and Boswell spent in each other's company, and one assumes that this deepened Boswell's knowledge of the man whose life he was to write. It was towards the end of the tour that Boswell records first having the idea of writing Johnson's life.

The Johnson of the *Tour*, however, represents an inter-mediate biographical statement; written in 1785, it comes after Johnson's death, and after the publication of Johnson's own version of their journey (*A Journey to the Western Islands of Scotland*) in 1775. It is also written with the consciousness that it is *not* to be the final statement about Samuel Johnson, and that it might therefore be freer to consider some aspects of Johnson's character and life without the burden of dealing with the meaning of his whole life in relation to his end. The Johnson of the *Tour*, though a man of great learning and moral stature, does not carry the same universal spiritual significance and seriousness, nor does he act and speak under the shadow of mortality as does the Johnson of the *Life*. Consequently, Boswell is far less self-conscious in the earlier work than he is in the later.

Nevertheless, Johnson's presence in Scotland is of great importance to Boswell: on one level it describes a process of 'Johnsonising' the land of Scotland – of bringing *the* great figure of the dominant English culture into a foreign land to test the mettle of both; on another level it represents a unification of Boswell's sensibility and psyche, in the coming together of the great nobles, Highland chiefs, and *literati* of Scotland with the great English man of letters, but particularly in the meeting of his father and Johnson at Auchinleck. Quite apart from the figure Johnson cuts in the work, the *Tour* is also filled with scenes from local Scots life and history, especially with the elegiac and romantic sentiments and memories of a defeated Jacobitism – history in which some of the people Boswell and Johnson met played a real part.

Unlike *Corsica*, the *Tour* follows a strict chronological structure. This is Boswell's narrative of Johnson's life while the *Life* is his portrait (Brady 84). Unlike the *Life*, the details and scenes of *Tour* remain relatively discrete, without fostering anything comparable to the reciprocity between particulars and the overriding idea of Johnson developed in the *Life*. The *Tour* begins with a detailed portrait of Johnson's character – one that later forms the basis of the concluding portrait of the *Life* (see chapter 4 below) – which Boswell portrays as fixed and autonomous, relatively unchanged by (though not indifferent to) his experience of the people and the landscape. The portrait fixes certain prominent physical, intellectual, and moral traits of Johnson in the mind of the reader from the start. It is with this collection of characteristics that Johnson is then depicted as sailing forth to encounter Scotland. The description is long but the following excerpt gives a powerful sense of Boswell's vision of Johnson:

Let my readers then remember that he was a sincere and zealous Christian, of high Church of England and monarchical principles, which he would not tamely suffer to be questioned; steady and inflexible in maintaining the obligations of piety and virtue, both from a regard to the order of society, and from a veneration for the Great Source of all order; correct, nay stern in his taste; hard to please, and easily offended, impetuous and irritable in his temper, but of a most humane and benevolent heart; having a mind stored with a vast and various collection of learning and knowledge, which he communicated with peculiar perspicuity and force, in rich and choice expression. He united a most logical head with a most fertile imagination, which gave him an extraordinary advantage in arguing; for he could reason close or wide, as he saw best for the moment. He could, when he chose it, be the greatest sophist that ever wielded a weapon in the schools of declamation... He was conscious of his superiority... He loved praise ... He was somewhat susceptible of flattery. His mind was so full of imagery, that he might have been perpetually a poet ... He had a constitutional melancholy, the clouds of which darkened the brightness of his fancy and gave a gloomy cast to his whole course of thinking ... He was prone to superstition but not to credulity ... He had a loud voice and a slow deliberate utterance ...

His person was large, robust, I may say approaching to the gigantick, and grown unwieldy from corpulency. His countenance was naturally of the cast of an ancient statue, but somewhat disfigured... He was now in his sixty-fourth year, and was become a little dull of hearing ... His head, and sometimes also his body, shook with a kind of motion like the effect of a palsy ... He wore a full suit of plain brown clothes, with twisted-hair buttons of the same colour, a large bushy greyish wig, a plain shirt, black worsted stockings, and silver buckles. Upon this tour, when journeying, he wore boots, and a very wide brown cloth great coat, with pockets which might have almost held the two volumes of his folio dictionary; and he carried in his hand a large English oak stick.   (163–5)

One remarkable aspect of this portrait is the coolness and simplicity of the details. Unlike the portrait in the *Life* (with which it is compared below, pp. 81–5), Boswell's style in the *Tour* is direct, spare, unencumbered by any covert interpretation of details. The first sentence of the passage operates paratactically, eschewing the conversational rhythms indicative of Boswell's prose for something more periodic and, perhaps, imitative of Johnson's style. The sentence begins with Johnson's Christian principles and it ends with his conversational expression, co-ordinates that might be said to encompass Johnson's whole way of being in Boswell's biographical enterprise. Though the parts of the sentence develop consecutively they are designed to work cumulatively, so that the momentary juxtaposition of God's order and Johnson's relatively petty demands ('Great Source of all order; correct, nay stern in his taste ...') is subsumed into a subtle unity represented by Johnson's 'most humane and benevolent heart', where, as it were, God is taken into humankind, softening and humanising one's foibles ('stern ... taste').

From this plateau the prose spreads outwards, invoking Johnson's characteristics arising from the moral unity enacted by the opening sentence – for example, 'logical head with a most fertile imagination'. Yet, as with other examples of Boswell's prose, this passage runs into difficulties of realisation, for the easy, ordered movement through the different levels of Johnson's life cannot generate the feel of what is being talked about – the relation between 'logical head' and 'fertile imagination' remains verbal, accurately, incisively verbal, but without a sense of what it feels like to put logic and imagination together. So the prose remains on the outside of Boswell's experience. All the subtle distinctions in the passage ('prone to superstition but not to credulity') point to essential elements in Johnson's character and way of being; but Boswell's idiom keeps them all in the same relation to himself. The levels of thought remain experientially separate.

Boswell's difficulty in transforming Johnson's mode of being into inner experience is peculiarly apt, for though the passage envisages Johnson as a great and impressive man, he is presented as existing within the material and historical realm; his countenance, his gestures, his clothing *mean* nothing other than what they are. Johnson's material existence is presented as being in harmony with his spiritual and intellectual life. This is not how Boswell portrays Johnson in the *Life*, where the moral grandeur is achieved in opposition to, and through a sublimation of, the material that Boswell implicitly claims to have a deep understanding of and sympathy for. The dignity of the portrait in the *Tour* lies more in its own and Johnson's pure unglamorous factualness: 'He wore a full suit of plain brown clothes, with twisted-hair buttons of the same colour ...' The passage, in fact, is remarkable for staving off the hint of the grotesque that is present in the proximity of grandeur and simplicity; as the image of the heroic ancient statue is qualified by the disfigurement of Johnson's appearance, so the grotesque is successfully channelled into the comic tone of the whole.

Johnson's 'oddness' is the focus of the *Tour*, and adds to its comedy. The fixed character envisaged in the opening is placed in a series of juxtapositions in unusual scenes throughout the work. But they do not develop the depth or complexity of Johnson's character just as they are not always flattering. But they do reveal him in action, and they also enhance the prominence of Boswell's character as he guides Johnson, acts as interpreter or observer, and as he sometimes explicitly stands out against his mentor. Both of these latter features are underplayed in the *Life*.

The entire experience of Johnson and Boswell in the Highlands and Hebrides might be considered as an extended juxta-position, exemplified, for example, by Boswell's surprise at finding civilised hospitality in a wild and barren place: 'I could not help being struck with some admiration, at finding upon this barren sandy point, such buildings, such a dinner, such company: it was like an enchantment' (227). There are also many particularly memorable scenes, such as the 'striking sight' of 'Dr Samuel Johnson, the great champion of the English Tories, salut[ing] Miss Flora Macdonald [of Jacobite fame] in the Isle of Sky' (265); the illiterate Highland guide attempting to entertain Johnson by whistling to make the goats jump (238); the sight of Johnson on horseback (230); and the occasion on which an old woman suspected Johnson of wanting to go to bed with her because he asked to see her bedroom (231).

In the *Tour*, unlike the *Life*, Boswell articulates his identity as being 'completely a citizen of the world', at home wherever he might be (166), and he stresses his ancient family, his own imagination and learning, and that he had internalised all Johnson's principles, 'with some degree of relaxation' (183). The narrative persona adopted in *Corsica* was one of a *naif*, in open and simple admiration of Paoli; in the *Tour* Boswell assumes an equality and familiarity with Johnson not explicit in the *Life*. This equality is emotionally rooted in Boswell's family and Scottish identity. On occasions he mentions how proud he is to be received as the son of his famous father, and enjoys having Johnson discover the ancient Scottish virtues in such a man as James Boyd, Earl of Errol: 'I saw in this nobleman the best dispositions and best principles; and I saw him, in my mind's eye, to be the representative of the ancient Boyds of Kilmarnock' (214; see 213–14). Boswell's pride in his cultural heritage balances Johnson's occasional stringent analysis of Scottish institutions such as the Presbyterian church, the Ossian poems, and Highland commerce. Sometimes Boswell's opposition takes the form of direct criticism of Johnson, as when he tells Johnson that he, Johnson, is ignorant of the Douglas cause (a significant lawsuit in eighteenth-century Scotland, in which Boswell acted for the orphaned Archibald Douglas in claiming the estates of his uncle, the Duke of Douglas – see Pottle, *Earlier Years* 311–17), and when he reflects on Johnson's lack of 'liberality' in abstaining from 'publick worship in our parish-church' at Auchinleck simply because it is presbyterian (398; also 384).

Brady writes that 'the quarrel between Johnson and Lord Auchinleck is the great unwritten scene in Boswell's journal' (80). The scene is unwritten for very good reasons. Boswell says, 'They became exceedingly warm, and violent, and I was very much distressed by being present at such an altercation between the two men, both of whom I reverenced; yet I durst not interfere. It would certainly be very unbecoming in me to exhibit my honoured father, and my respected friend, as intellectual gladiators, for the entertainment of the publick ...' (397–8). Boswell feels responsible for both men, yet powerless to effect the reconciliation between the representatives of two cultures and between different sides of his own psyche, which the *Tour* artistically enacts. In one way the *Tour* is a written recognition of Boswell's father, who had died in 1782, insofar as it embraces Boswell's connections with the culture of which his father was a significant representative. But despite these connections, the love that Boswell feels for his father is fraught with anxiety, feelings which he attempts to propitiate metonymically and symbolically in his life and his writing. The father was unable and unwilling, as Johnson was not, to be used as a figure in relation to whom Boswell could define himself.

That process of definition, however, changes from the *Tour* to the *Life*. While the *Tour* maintains a sense of Johnson's separateness — perhaps made more possible for Boswell by Johnson's existence in the context of a real father and a real Scotland — it also suggests how easy it was for Boswell to appropriate the object of his interest:

I was elated by the thought of having been able to entice such a man to this remote part of the world. A ludicrous, yet just image presented itself to my mind ... I compared myself to a dog who has got hold of a large piece of meat, and runs away with it to a corner, where he may devour it in peace, without any fear of others taking it from him. 'In London, Reynolds, Beauclerk, and all of them, are contending who shall enjoy Dr Johnson's conversation. We are feasting upon it, undisturbed, at Dunvegan.' (286)

The process of injestion and recreation metaphorically described here is more fully effected in the *Life*. While Boswell's father is acknowledged and released in the *Tour*, Boswell's surrogate father — the antithesis of the real father in terms of principles and temperament — is thoroughly internalised in the *Life*. The interiority of the imaginative world of the *Life* (despite all the factual and historical elements of that work) is central to its effectiveness as biography and artifact, and is of the essence of the work's modern sensibility. It has been implicitly praised by critics as a necessary part of Boswell's artifice, and it has completely convinced many readers that Boswell's portrayal of Johnson is historically accurate.

Although *Corsica* and the *Tour* are preparatory works for the *Life*, and though they are both considered consciously crafted works according to their own purposes, they are not of the same kind as the *Life*. The sympathetic attention to character, the structure of the work, and, particularly, the dynamic relationship between Boswell and Johnson in the *Life*, differentiate it from Boswell's other works.

Chapter 4

The structure, scenes, and conversations of the *Life*

Structurally the *Life* operates on three levels at once: there is the explicit chronological structure that runs from Johnson's birth in 1709 to his death in 1784; there is the thematic structure which focuses on certain significant moments in Johnson's life, such as the meeting with George III, or with Boswell himself. There is also the symbolic structure expressed in the portrait of Johnson's character which derives from the many accumulated particular moments in the *Life*, and which is also the expression of Boswell's artistic idea of Johnson – of Johnson's personal, metaphoric, and cultural–political significance. Because Boswell's vision of Johnson is artistic and not merely documentary, his portrait of Johnson's character paradoxically both precedes and results from the act and experience of writing the biography – it is something Boswell both discovers in and brings to his encounter with Johnson. The book does not place much importance on chronology *per se*, or on the equal distribution of space and attention to the different parts of Johnson's life. Paul Alkon has demonstrated how Boswell's narrative slows down the tempo of the chronology at certain times so that the narrative time (the time taken to read certain passages) parallels and gives the impression of 'real', historical time, so that Johnson can (metaphorically) be kept in the present. This is one of the reasons why some years in Johnson's life are allotted very few pages, while others receive hundreds (for example, 1758 gets ten pages while 1775, 1776, and 1778 get 93, 126, and 120 pages respectively). The first fifty-four years of Johnson's life – the period before Boswell met Johnson – is dealt with in 271 pages in the World's Classics edition; the period from 1763 to 1784 runs from page 271 to page 1402. Most of the biography is devoted to the last ten years of Johnson's life, that is, from the tour of Scotland

40

(when Boswell announced his intention of writing this biography) to Johnson's death.

There are other apparent anomalies. Greene has pointed out how few days (no more than 425) between 1763 and 1784 were actually spent by Boswell in Johnson's company (''Tis a Pretty Book, Mr Boswell' 132–42). A hundred and one of those days are accounted for by the Scottish tour of 1773, which, in fact, find no place in the *Life* since the *Tour* constitutes for Boswell a 'separate and remarkable portion' of Johnson's life (553), and has in any case been dealt with in the earlier publication. This 'disjointed and unbalanced narrative' (Waingrow 45), however, does not necessarily weaken Boswell's book, since Boswell's purpose is not primarily documentary but, as Alkon, Dowling and others have recognised, imaginative and recreative. Boswell uses his memos and journal entries of Johnson's actions and *bons mots* imaginatively, and aims to recreate an authentic image of Johnson that captures his essence. Many readers of the *Life* still mistake Boswell's depiction of Johnson's conversations for the actual words and actual form spoken by the historical Samuel Johnson. But this is not so, and Boswell notifies the reader both explicitly and implicitly that he is *recreating* his image of Johnson from historical material. Perhaps anticipating criticism of his factual knowledge of Johnson, and wishing to separate his book from a mere chronicle, Boswell acknowledges that his record of Johnson's conversation is not entire, or literally accurate in every detail; but 'what I have preserved ... has the *value* of the most perfect authenticity' (617; also 403–4, 599). For Boswell, authenticity is an inner experience and the result of his artistic reconstruction – his fiction – of the structure and reality of Johnson's life (Clingham, 'Truth and Artifice').

In this, Boswell's book shares something essential with J.-J. Rousseau's autobiographical enterprise. As Jean Starobinski demonstrates (*Transparency and Obstruction*, trans. A. Goldhammer (Chicago, 1971), 198–200), Rousseau's *Confessions* (1782–9) and the *Reveries of the Solitary Walker* (1782) developed a form of 'authentic speech' about himself that is not limited to imitation of historical facts, against which his text would have to be verified, but which is free to deform and invent imaginatively, so long as he remains faithful to his own inner feeling in the present moment. For Rousseau, the self that is the object of his autobiography is not given but is created in the act of writing. Historical truth becomes authentic discourse. As with Boswell, for Rousseau language becomes a locus of immediate experience, even while it is an instrument of historical mediation. It is the instrument of authenticity, shaping a personal feeling rooted in the imaginative sympathy and understanding he feels he has with Johnson: 'In progress of time, when my mind was, as it were, *strongly impregnated with the Johnsonian aether*, I could, with much more facility and exactness, carry in my memory and commit to paper the exuberant variety of his wisdom and wit' (297).

As a description of artistic recreation, Boswell's words are quite appropriate: his dramatisation of Johnson's life and the portrait of Johnson's character that emerges use documentary evidence, including many of Johnson's letters, which give a direct view into Johnson's heart and mind, illustrating, in various contexts, his generosity, tenderness, practicality, good sense, and wide knowledge. But the biography is given a cutting edge by virtue of Boswell's artistic, fictional recreation of Johnson. It is this which impresses Macaulay so strongly, and which has sustained the praise of coherence and self-consistency expressed by modern critics. In keeping with this scheme, the most imaginative compelling parts of the *Life* are extended conversations and scenes in which Johnson is depicted as engaging with others and manifesting his essential qualities. Boswell's dramatic method focuses the reader's attention on discrete, vivid, immediate episodes through which Johnson's character is developed. There are many 'scenes' exemplifying Boswell's dramatic prose – some from before, but mainly from after, he met Johnson. Boswell's meeting with Johnson in Davies's bookshop (272–9), Johnson accompanying Boswell to Harwich on his journey to Holland (327), Johnson's meeting with King George III in the library at the Queen's House in 1767 (379–84), Boswell dining with Johnson at Easter, 1773 (511–12), Johnson at a dinner party with

John Wilkes in 1776 (764–76), Johnson in conversation with Oliver Edwards in 1778, forty-nine years after they had been freshmen at Pembroke College, Oxford (955–9), and the death-bed scene, are only some of the many memorable formal 'scenes' in the *Life*. On many occasions – such as at the dinner party at the home of Sir Joshua Reynolds on 9 April 1778 (915–23); at the Mitre tavern, other inns, and at the homes of people such as the Thrales and Reynolds; involving such friends as Garrick, Burke, Goldsmith, Burney, Langton, and Beauclerk – Johnson is pictured in conversation with a wide range of people from the world of literature, law, and politics, and from almost every other branch of eighteenth-century culture.

One scene worth citing for its dramatic skill, as well as being an indication of Johnson's energy and spirit, took place in 1752, before Boswell met Johnson:

One night when Beauclerk and Langton had supped at a tavern in London, and sat till about three in the morning, it came into their heads to go and knock up Johnson, and see if they could prevail on him to join them in a ramble. They rapped violently at the door of his chambers in the Temple, till at last he appeared in his shirt, with his little black wig on the top of his head, instead of a nightcap, and a poker in his hand, imagining, probably, that some ruffians were coming to attack him. When he discovered who they were, and was told their errand, he smiled, and with great good humour agreed to their proposal: 'What, is it you, you dogs! I'll have a frisk with you.' He was soon drest, and they sallied forth together into Covent-Garden, where the greengrocers and fruiterers were beginning to arrange their hampers, just come in from the country. (176)

This little episode testifies to Boswell's ability to dramatise a complex scene in simple, clear prose so as to convey the texture and feel of the scene. We have the excited energy of the revellers, and Johnson's generous response to their high spirits, as well as little physical details catching Johnson's gesture and accent, in the midst of his life – the wig and the poker comically suggesting his eccentricity and courage. The ubiquitous, authenticating background presence of London life is particularised by the ruffians coming to attack Johnson (something Boswell probably imagined Johnson as thinking, rather than getting this motive for his appearance from either Johnson or his companions), and the early-morning market life in Covent Garden. Most convincing, perhaps, is the single piece of direct speech Boswell provides in this passage: it adds life and immediacy to the sketch, and catches the inflexion of real speech (different from the formal Johnson that one commonly associates with Boswell). The direct speech also suggests the spirited generosity and good humour of Johnson's character and his friendship with these two men younger than himself. In another key, the same may be said of the tiny qualifier to Johnson's response, 'he smiled'. Stylistically it is almost invisible, and yet it registers both Johnson's physical and spiritual being in the passage.

It is likely that Boswell supplied both the form and the words for Johnson's behaviour on this occasion not from a detailed account from any of the participants, but from his own imagination, based on a general report of what had happened. The scene conveys the pleasure of a fully formed artistic vignette, and thus of having captured the truth. Pottle says, 'Johnson's conversation as Boswell reported it, is, for all its veridicality, an imaginative construction; it is embedded in a narrative made continuously lively by unobtrusive specks of imagination' ('Art and Authenticity' 72). The sprightliness of Boswell's narrative on this occasion is matched by many at which he was present, such as the (quite ordinary) dinner he and Johnson share at Mrs Garrick's home in 1781, which he describes as 'one of the happiest days that I remember to have enjoyed in the whole course of my life' (1139).

Boswell perceives Johnson's conversation as peculiarly revealing of Johnson the man, and 'perhaps, [as] more admirable than even his writings, however excellent' (1101). He was not alone in this perception. Hogarth recommended Johnson to Mrs Thrale's acquaintance because his conversation was the talk of other people (*JM* 240), and Mrs Thrale notes, penetratingly, that talk was so essential to Johnson's being that 'To recollect ... and to repeat the sayings of Johnson, is almost all that can be done by the writers of his life'(*JM* 160). It is on a dramatic embodiment of that principle that Boswell predicates the success of his biography. Conversation is a central, cohering aspect of the work: 'What I consider as the peculiar value of the following work, is, the quantity that it contains of Johnson's conversation; which is universally acknowledged to have been eminently instructive and entertaining ... the conversation of a celebrated man, if his talents have been exerted in conversation, will best display his character ...' (23). Again, Boswell says 'I cannot conceive a more perfect mode of writing any man's life, than not only relating all the more important events of it in their order, but interweaving what he privately wrote, and said, and thought; by which mankind are enabled as it were to see him live, and to "live o'er each scene" with him, as he actually advanced through the several stages of his life' (22).

However, precisely because of Boswell's artistic selectivity in dramatising Johnson's conversation, his accuracy has become contentious. Greene has demonstrated how some of Boswell's more 'creative' renditions of Johnson's 'sayings' do not accurately portray either Johnson's words or his meaning, and so present a false view of Johnson's actual position, that has prejudiced the understanding of him as a man and writer. Among Boswell's 'creative substitutions' is such a famous 'Johnsonian' statement as, 'The woman's a whore, and there's an end on't', which makes Greene question the very concept of 'sayings' as we have them, as characteristically Johnsonian ('*Logia* of Johnson' 4).

At the same time, many contemporaries corroborate Boswell's view of the tone of Johnson's conversation – the 'extraordinary vigour', the 'roughness of manner' with the absence of 'ill-nature in his disposition' (279). Boswell makes a point of opposing the impression he thinks Mrs Thrale's *Anecdotes* give of Johnson's 'constitutional irritability of temper': 'his time was chiefly spent in instructing and delighting mankind by his writings and conversation, in acts of piety to God, and good-will to men' (290–1). On one occasion Boswell expresses the sheer fun and delight of 'chatting' with Johnson: 'During this interview at Ashbourne, Johnson and I frequently talked with wonderful pleasure of mere trifles which had occurred in our tour of the Hebrides' (872). Many record (in Boswell's words) the 'extraordinary power and precision of [Johnson's] conversation' (284). Some remark on his 'loud voice, and ... slow deliberate utterance' with which he enforced the 'elegant choice of language' (1402). Even Johnson's tendency in the *Life* to speak aphoristically (a 'Johnsonese' that many Johnsonians are beginning to suspect of being more Boswell than Johnson) even this touches on one of Johnson's more memorable and penetrating stylistic habits: we remember, 'The true Genius is a mind of large general powers, accidentally determined to some particular direction', from the 'Life of Cowley', and, from the 'Life of Milton', 'we are perpetually moralists, but we are geometricians only by chance', and many others. Hawkins notes that 'As [Johnson] professed always to speak in the best and most correct phrase ... his conversation style bore a great resemblance to that of his writings' (163).

Nevertheless, artistic recreation – fictionalising – and appropriation are what Boswell is engaged in. The immediacy of which he speaks as the purpose of his particular biographical method is imaginative; of course, the reader does not actually live over each scene with Johnson, but Boswell's dramatic technique makes it feel as if we do. The authenticity of his portrait – and, hence, the suggestiveness of its 'truth' – are enhanced by his inclusion of Johnson's aggression and irritability, and his talking for the purpose of 'winning' an argument. For since Johnson's life was not 'entirely perfect', he will take into account the 'shade as well as light [by] ... delineat[ing] him without reserve' (22).

Whatever Boswell's accuracy in depicting Johnson's historical conversation, by focusing on conversation Boswell hit upon an essential element in Johnson's soul, for conversation was to Johnson a mode of being and action that entailed a moral engagement with others, with the world, with self, and even with God. In the *Dictionary* Johnson quotes Dryden to illustrate the sense of conversation as 'commerce, intercourse, familiarity': 'The knowledge of men and manners, the freedom of habititudes, and conversation with the best company'. Waingrow notes that talk may also have touched Johnson's melancholia, as both a source and a balm of anxiety (48). It is certainly true that talk took these forms for Boswell, and in assessing the *Life of Johnson* it is necessary to distinguish between what Johnson thought important for himself and what Boswell thought was important to him. Feeling that he is peculiarly sensitive to the 'Johnsonian aether' − something that made him feel 'elevated as if brought into another state of being' and even, momentarily, made him feel at one with Mrs Thrale (680) − leads Boswell to believe that he can read Johnson's mind, to know what Johnson *would have said*: 'It is amazing how a mimick can not only give you the gestures and voice of a person whom he represents; but even what a person would say on any particular subject' (465). The practical consequences of this insight are twofold: they affect Boswell's status as a narrator and his relationship to Johnson within the world of the *Life*; and they influence the quality and content of the portrait of Johnson given by Boswell. Boswell's working from within the supposition that he knows Johnson so inwardly that he knows what he *would* say and think underscores the dramatic rendition of Johnson, but it also shapes Boswell's appropriation of Johnson. Boswell's artistic treatment of Johnson, and his sympathy, mean in practice that he understands Johnson largely in terms of himself, and that he enlists Johnson's authority in support of his own preoccupations. This practice constitutes both the strength and the weakness of the *Life*, and is what convinces such critics as Donald Greene and Richard Schwartz of the weakness of the *Life* as biography, and persuades others, such as Ralph Rader and William Dowling, of its strength as artifice and fiction.

Comparison between the Journals (featuring Johnson) and the *Life* generally reveal a movement away from documentary reporting to a more sophisticated dramatic presentation of character. Corresponding to this is a movement from overt personal involvement on Boswell's part to a more artistically fashioned, detached narrative persona. I have already mentioned the example of the parting between Boswell and Johnson before Boswell leaves for Holland in 1763, as an example in which Boswell depersonalises the version in the *Life* by eliminating his tears (see above, p. 21). Another small example is in order here. The Journal for 1772 was heavily used as a basis for the *Life*. On 31 March 1772 the two men discussed hospitality. In transcribing the scene from the Journal to the *Life*, Boswell removes the more personal vulnerable comment from the later work, and rephrases his opening to provide more distance. In the Journal we have, 'I consulted him whether a man should lay himself out to show great hospitality. This was an important subject for me who would naturally go to an excess of hospitality, both from inclination and from a notion that it makes a man of great consequence' (*Defence* 84). The *Life* has, only, 'I asked him how far he thought wealth should be employed in hospitality' (475). The Journal reveals the personal application of the question for Boswell, while the *Life* is more restrained and distanced. There are many examples of these small but important 'translations' when comparing the *Life* with the Journal for 1769–74, *Boswell for the Defence*.

Nonetheless, this distancing does not mean that Boswell is not personally involved in narrating the *Life*, although that is the initial impression. Boswell's feelings are internalised and permitted to shape the subtle interpretations he gives to Johnson's actions and words. That is, instead of responding to an independent person, with a degree of incomprehensible otherness, outside the self, Boswell 'sympathetically' and 'imaginatively' incorporates Johnson, and recreates that external phenomenon, that Other, in his own image. 'In creating the *Life* … Boswell was in a real sense creating an objective correlative of a grand emotive idea. His idea was not so much an aid to him in his task as it was the very principle of that astonishing reconstruction' (Rader 29). The distance between Boswell and Johnson – the historical differences between, say, the 1750s (when Johnson was writing the *Rambler*) and the 1790s (when Boswell was writing the *Life*), and the different philosophical substance to Johnson's writing – these are collapsed into Boswell's interior world. Readers tend to think that this collapsing is a precondition for the finished work of art, or the operation of genuine sympathy; but whatever identification the imaginative *process* might entail, in the *end* the collapsing of the space and boundaries between Boswell and Johnson generates its own doubt, and melancholia for Boswell.

The anxiety associated with self-definition, power, control, and sexual pleasure in Boswell's relationship with Louisa is also present in the *Life* in Boswell's relationship with Johnson, only now it is translated into a form of art higher than that of the *London Journal*. This human predicament underlies the importance of the constructed, imagined relation between Boswell and Johnson in the structure of the *Life*. Almost every memorable and vivid scene in the book incorporates a Boswell–Johnson personal axis, an emotional, psychological, spiritual, or intellectual spark between the two. Sometimes this is quite appropriate, such as on the occasion (in 1777) on which the two of them 'stood in calm conference by [them]selves in Dr Taylor's garden, at a pretty late hour in a serene autumn night, looking up to the heavens', and with Johnson in a 'placid and most benignant frame', when Boswell was able to 'direct the discourse to the subject of a future state' (875). Sometimes, however, Boswell uses Johnson as a sounding-board, generating a significance for Johnson only insofar as Boswell responds to him; and, vice versa, generating a sense of personal purpose insofar as Johnson responds to Boswell. From this point of view the uneven disposition of space and time in the book sugggests that Johnson is less important to Boswell when he, Boswell, is not present in London or in Johnson's circle. When Boswell is historically absent from the narration Johnson's presence becomes nominally weaker and he seems less significant for Boswell. This proposition is borne out in many particular instances.

Thus Boswell's account of Johnson's attempt to save Dr William Dodd from the gallows (for forgery) is placed in the section after 15 September 1777, where, Boswell says, it 'is the proper place to give an account of Johnson's humane and zealous interference in behalf of the Reverend Dr William Dodd' (827). But Dodd had been hanged on 27 June 1777, at a time when Boswell was in Edinburgh (in September 1777 he was with Johnson in Ashbourne). Even though Johnson had written to Boswell about Dodd's death on 28 June 1777 (Boswell prints the letter on pages 811–13), Boswell evidently found the event less compelling when he was unable to imagine himself in the presence of Johnson. I say 'imagine' because, of course, in 1785–91, when Boswell was writing the *Life*, *everything* in Johnson's life was in the past, and could only be recollected; so Boswell could have placed the event anywhere, and have made it equally interesting. But Dodd was to Johnson a little like Reid was to Boswell, and perhaps Boswell's identification with Johnson's humane efforts (against all the legal odds and customs) was so strong that he inevitably envisaged himself in close proximity.

Johnson's otherness, Johnson's humour

How Boswell deals with Johnson's otherness is central to the *Life*. Sometimes Johnson's actions do not fit Boswell's expectation, his idea of what Johnson *should* be doing, or what he '*would say* on [any one] particular subject'. For 10 May 1773 Boswell writes:

I have known him at times exceedingly diverted at what seemed to others a very small sport. He now laughed immoderately, without any reason that we could perceive, at our friend's [Langton] making his will; called him the *testator*, and added, 'I dare say, he thinks he has done a mighty thing. He won't stay till he gets home to his seat in the country, to produce this wonderful deed: he'll call up the landlord of the first inn on the road; and, after a suitable preface upon mortality and the uncertainty of life, will tell him that he should not delay making his will; and here, Sir, will he say, is my will, which I have just made, with the assistance of one of the ablest lawyers in the kingdom; and he will read it to him (laughing all the time). He believes he has made this will; but he did not make it: you, Chambers, made it for him. I trust you have had more conscience than to make him say, "being of sound understanding"; ha, ha, ha! I hope he has left me a legacy. I'd have his will turned into verse, like a ballad.'

   In this playful manner did he run on, exulting in his own pleasantry, which certainly was not such as might be expected from the author of *The Rambler*, but which is here preserved, that my readers may be acquainted even with the slightest occasional characteristicks of so eminent a man.   (548–9)

Not quite able to make sense of this event, Boswell does what for him is the next best thing — and what, at the same time, makes him a sensitive biographer: he recreates Johnson's actions and words as if they were part of a novel. Once again, this passage gives us not the studied formality of the conventional 'Johnsonian' 'saying' or aphorism, but the immediate direct speech, and the flexible, supple accents of the spoken voice in the heat of the moment. Boswell captures a remarkable range of tone, from the potential severity and truculence of 'I dare say, he thinks he has done a mighty thing ...', to the studied parody of 'and here, Sir, will he say, is my will', to the Rabelaisian laughter ('ha, ha, ha! I hope he has left me a legacy') that dissolves the innocent pretentiousness and myth making underlying this example of the vanity of human wishes. At the same time, Boswell articulates the sympathy that Johnson must have felt in imagining Langton on his picaresque journey, a kind of Parson Adams. The whole episode captures a very Johnsonian mixture of sarcasm and human sympathy.

But Johnson's behaviour is not as uncharacteristic as Boswell appears to think when he offers this episode as an example of the 'slightest characteristick of so eminent a man'. There seems to be a tension between Johnson's laughter and what Boswell sees as appropriate behaviour for the author of the *Rambler*, and this tension is mirrored in the tonal shift between the direct speech and Boswell's mildly disapproving comment that follows. The division raises the question as to whether Boswell's novelistic presentation appreciates the fineness of the Johnsonian humour that it captures so effortlessly. Johnson, of course, is laughing at the folly of human aspirations and fantasies in the face of mortality, but he is laughing in a profoundly sympathetic way and understanding those frailties. His use of the word 'testator', for example, echoes the imagined greatness and specialness that Langton's will-making generates, and draws attention to the difference between human actions and the garb in which people attempt to dress them up. The word 'testator' is a big Johnsonian word, but deliberately and ironically used, so that the reader or auditor can feel the discrepancy between Langton's self-importance and the simple act of making a will.

However, Langton's will-making also testifies to a person's need to plan, to make a bulwark against the inevitable – using the human institution of the law to assure oneself of safety, and of control of the reality of mortality that admits only of uncertainty and the uncontrollable. But the moment is neither simply about the greatness nor about the littleness of humankind, for Johnson's laughter dissolves any easy and strict opposition *or* identity between these two entities. Somewhere between 'mortality and the uncertainty of life' and the act of having a famous lawyer draw up a will, lies, for Johnson, a profound, paradoxical connection between what one *must* do to maintain purpose and functionality, and what one *must* do to surrender to the temporal process in life necessary for spiritual self-possession, trust, and growth. The connection between those experiential imperatives can only be acknowledged by laughter: a laughter that is, perhaps, richer for the knowledge that Sir Robert Chambers's fame as the Vinerian Professor of Law at Oxford was facilitated by Johnson's helping him write more than sixty lectures on the law. Equally, Johnson's is a laughter that accepts the inevitability of mortality, and simultaneously raises the participant to a level at which he is able to embrace what is usually too difficult to face. This is a deeply natural moment for Johnson. He seems to experience something like the greatness-in-littleness and the littleness-in-greatness that characterises Falstaff, the character who Johnson thought epitomised Shakespeare's dramatic capacity for the natural: 'Thou compound of sense and vice; of sense which may be admired but not esteemed, of vice which may be despised, but hardly detested' (*Johnson on Shakespeare*, ed. A. Sherbo, Intro. B. Bronson, 2 vols. (Yale, 1968), 523 (pagination consecutive in the 2 vols.)). This scene also shows that side of Johnson that made him such an admirer of Erasmus's *In Praise of Folly* and of Dryden's *Fables*.

Boswell's prose captures a haunting sense of existential loneliness in Johnson's laughter:

Johnson could not stop his merriment, but continued it all the way till we got without the Temple-gate. He then burst into such a fit of laughter, that he appeared to be almost in a convulsion; and, in order to support himself, laid hold of one of the posts at the side of the foot pavement, and sent forth peals so loud, that in the silence of the night his voice seemed to resound from Temple-bar to Fleet-ditch.   (549)

The unnerving feel of the moment for Boswell is captured in the images – the 'silence of the night' placed against Johnson's largeness and his being out of control, in the grip of something irrational ('convulsion'). The hyperbole – his voice resounding the whole length of London – moves away from burlesque towards nightmare, or something Gothic, by the gravity of the energy.

For all the sensitivity of the prose, however, Boswell seems unaware that Johnson's laughter is about loneliness and death. Loneliness and death are, of course, two of the great topics of conversation in the *Life*, but Boswell invariably assumes that because they were subjects of great seriousness for Johnson, the author of the *Rambler would* only deal with them in a solemn, fearful, and melancholy way. For Boswell, Johnson's eminence is directly linked to his way of dealing with questions of death, the afterlife, and divine judgement in both his writing and his private life. Boswell frequently brings up these questions because they are of compelling, sometimes obsessive interest to himself, and the silent agenda of his 'conversation' with Johnson on these topics is the urgent need for emotional and spiritual assurance and comfort. Often Boswell's anxieties about annihilation and the inability to know for sure what the afterlife holds are associated with Hume's philosophy and his attitudes to death (see chapter 5, pp. 97–103 below).

On one occasion (26 October 1769) when Boswell brings up Hume's declaration that he was untroubled by the thought that he would not exist after life, Johnson accuses Hume of madness or falsity, but follows that up with a more telling observation that 'When he [Hume] dies, he at least gives up all he has' (426). For Johnson, the possibility that Hume could face death with as much detachment as he claimed, if it annihilates all human connections and pleasure, seriously impugns his humanity, however it might strengthen his philosophical position. To part from life without *any* trouble is evidence to Johnson that Hume has no human connections, that he is not *in* life at all. But Boswell does not take this up. He wants to know whether we may 'not fortify our minds for the approach of death?' (427). This question, however, he feels is 'wrong' because it brought 'before [Johnson's] view what he ever looked upon with horrour'. Then Boswell makes a famous comparison of Johnson and his fears to a gladiator combating wild beasts:

His mind resembled the vast amphitheatre, the Colisaeum at Rome. In the centre stood his judgement, which, like a mighty gladiator, combated those apprehensions that, like the wild beats of the *Arena*, were all around in cells, ready to be let out upon him. After a conflict, he drove them back into their dens; but not killing them, they were still assailing him.   (427)

Boswell's images depict one aspect of what he saw as Johnson's heroism: the parallel between the isolated, courageous, and morally grand Johnson fighting off the threats of a hostile world, and the mind having to deal with the threats to its sanity produced from within. Johnson's aggressive relation to the world is a metaphor for his relation to himself. Fear of death, by implication, is a wild beast, and comes out of Johnson's unconscious to assail him from time to time. Yet the images also suggest the enormous, monumental achievement in Johnson's battles with his inner demon, for they conjure up cultural memories of the origins of Christianity (the naked Christian at the mercy of the Romans now becomes the 'mighty gladiator'), and such intellectual efforts as Gibbon's *Decline and Fall of the Roman Empire*, conceived in Rome: 'It was at Rome, on the 15th of October, 1764, as I sat musing amidst the ruins of the Capitol, while the barefooted friars were singing vespers in the Temple of Jupiter, that the idea of writing the decline and fall of the city first started to my mind' (*Autobiography of Edward Gibbon*, ed. J.B. Bury (Oxford, 1962), 160). Boswell's extended metaphor is so striking that it carries with it the conviction of the truth; many modern critics of Johnson – W. J. Bate, for example – have taken this inner psychological and spiritual struggle expressed in Boswell's prose as the starting point from which to discuss Johnson's mind. But on this occasion the imagery with which Boswell presents Johnson may be determined as much by his own fears of death as they are by Johnson's. For Johnson's response to Boswell's question exhibits nothing of the gladiator; he is tetchy and, as Boswell says, 'in a passion', but this, I suggest, is because Boswell's focus is morbid and not because Johnson is particularly horrified: '"No, Sir, let it alone. It matters not how a man dies, but how he lives. The act of dying is not of importance, it lasts so short a time." He added, (with an earnest look,) "A man knows it must be so, and submits. It will do him no good to whine"' (427).

Boswell seems unable to detect the tone of Johnson's response (exasperation, defensiveness), nor does he respond to Johnson's *thought* – the distinction and the connection between living and dying, and the freedom that can be had from living in the moment but with consciousness of a teleology beyond the present. Boswell tries to continue the conversation, but Johnson becomes agitated and passionate, and finally asks to be left alone on that occasion and the following day: he 'called to me [Boswell] sternly, "Don't let us meet to-morrow"' (427). Boswell is unable to honour this claim to privacy; he rehearses all the 'harsh observations ... made upon [Johnson's] character', then sends Johnson a note complaining of his severity and asking for reconciliation. Having insistently brought up a topic on which he knows Johnson to be sensitive, and having failed to detect what Johnson was actually saying in response to his questions, Boswell is unable to deal with the consequences and the feelings that arise from the encounter. So (in his mind) he first punishes Johnson, then seeks oneness. He gets himself in this position because he is more concerned with his own horror of death, and with *his* feelings of distress arising from Johnson's action of separating himself.

What Boswell feels as Johnson's indifference to his anxiety is his single greatest complaint in the *Life*, and, like an aggrieved lover or one set on ignoring his own vulnerability, Boswell repeatedly refuses to accept the consolation Johnson *does* offer in letters and in his particular way of dealing with the questions Boswell raises: 'It matters not how a man dies, but how he lives.' This tough wisdom, focusing on the present moment and distinguishing between what one must accept and what one can change, perhaps leads Boswell to think (as he does) that Johnson does not appreciate pathos in literature. They differ consistently on the merits of the poetry of Gray, Mason, and the Scottish sentimentalists, and when Johnson discussed Young's *Night Thoughts* in the 'Life of Young', Boswell was in much trepidation that he would not do justice to the exquisite sentiment of the poem: 'there is in this Poem not only all that Johnson so well brings in view, but a power of the *Pathetick* beyond almost any example that I have seen. He who does not feel his nerves shaken, and his heart pierced by many passages in this extraordinary work ... must be of a hard and obstinate frame' (1111). Certainly, Boswell's observation that in Johnson's works 'there is not a single passage that ever drew a tear' (1098) suggests that he did not think that Johnson had the requisite capacity for the pathetic to appreciate *Night Thoughts*. As it is, Johnson's understanding of the pathetic as 'that uniformity of sentiment, which enables us to conceive and to excite the pains and pleasures of other minds' ('Life of Cowley', *Lives of the English Poets*, ed. G. B. Hill, 3 vols. (Oxford, 1905), I, 20) enables him to connect Boswell's capacity for strong feelings and impressionableness with the loss of self and confidence accompanying predestination: 'Do not, Sir', he said to Boswell, 'accustom yourself to trust to *impressions*. There is a middle state of mind between conviction and hypocrisy, of which many are conscious. By trusting to impressions, a man may gradually come to yield to them, and at length be subject to them, so as not to be a free agent, or what is the same thing in effect, to *suppose* that he is not a free agent' (1159).

That middle state, the distinction Johnson makes between what one can change and what one must accept, is the space inhabited by Johnson's moral presence, but it is a space (and a silence) that Boswell frequently needs to fill up with questions and feelings. In response to Boswell's persistent need to use language to eliminate difference and space, Johnson wrote to him in 1776: 'I am very sorry that your melancholy should return, and should be sorry likewise if it could have no relief but from company ... Do not ... hope wholly to reason away your troubles; do not feed them with attention, and they will die imperceptibly away. Fix your thoughts upon your business, fill your intervals with company, and sunshine will again break in upon your mind' (676).

Laughter is a kind of sunshine, and, in the face of the *inevitability* of mortality, a great affirmation of life. Boswell is divided on Johnson's humour, even though, at the end of the *Life*, he affirms the 'uncommon and peculiar powers of [Johnson's] wit and humour', and describes their effects in terms reminiscent of Johnson's description of Falstaff: 'he frequently indulged himself in colloquial pleasantry; and the heartiest merriment was often enjoyed in his company; with this great advantage, that as it was entirely free from any poisonous tincture of vice or impiety, it was salutary to those who shared in it' (1401). Given this general recognition at the end of the *Life*, it is unusual and significant that Boswell remains relatively obtuse when it comes to particular events in which Johnson himself (rather than Boswell, as in the Wilkes episode, discussed on pp. 61–78) is making the comedy.

Alongside the bellicose, serious Johnson we often meet in Boswell's pages there is also a very funny and good-humoured Johnson. Many of his contemporaries testified to his humour, including Sir John Hawkins (1719–89), Mrs Hester Thrale Piozzi (1741–1821), Frances Burney (1752–1840), Arthur Murphy (1727–1805), and Hannah More (1745–1833). These individuals were members of Johnson's 'circle' at various times during his life. More was an educationalist and a member of the Blue Stocking Circle; Murphy was a barrister, journalist, actor, and dramatist, and later (1792) one of Johnson's biographers; Burney was the daughter of Dr Charles Burney (musicologist and composer, and one of Johnson's closest friends), author of *Evelina* and other novels, and later became Mme D'Arblay, under which name she published her extensive diaries.

Mrs Thrale and Sir John Hawkins are more important figures in Johnson's life. Mrs Thrale (nee Salusbury) was Johnson's intimate friend from 1764, soon after she had married Henry Thrale, brewer and MP for Southwark. From 1765 Johnson had his own room at Streatham, their home in Surrey, where he spent happy hours in conversation with the Thrales and friends, and he also accompanied them to Wales (1774) and France (1775). After Mr Thrale's death in 1781, a rift developed between Johnson and Mrs Thrale, exacerbated by her liaison with and then marriage to Gabriel Piozzi (1784), an Italian musician. Hawkins was an attorney, magistrate, and musician. He was knighted in 1772 for his duties as a magistrate. He published a *History of Music* in 1776 (unfavourably compared with Charles Burney's History which appeared in the same year), and his edition of Johnson's works in eleven volumes in 1787–9, including the *Life* as volume I. Hawkins became acquainted with Johnson through Edward Cave (proprietor of *The Gentleman's Magazine*, for which Johnson wrote in his early years). He was among the nine initial members of a club started by Johnson in 1748–9 at the King's Head in Ivy Lane, and a member of the famous Club formed in 1763. Johnson is reported by Frances Burney as saying of Hawkins that 'he is penurious and he is mean, and it must be owned he has a degree of brutality and a tendency to savageness that cannot easily be defended' (*Diary* (1875), I, 65). Despite this view Johnson permitted Hawkins to draw up his will in 1784, and made him one of his executors, a position of honour resented by Boswell.

Hawkins was no *bon vivant*, so his comments on Johnson's humour are interesting. He notes: Johnson

was a great contributor to the mirth of conversation, by the many witty sayings he uttered, and the many excellent stories which his memory had treasured up, and he would on occasion relate; so that those are greatly mistaken who infer, either from the general tendency of his writings, or that appearance of hebetude which marked his countenance when living, and is discernible in the pictures and prints of him, that he could only reason and discuss, dictate and controul.

(110–11)

Mrs Thrale, too, is decisive in announcing that

Dr Johnson was not grave ... because he knew not how to be merry.
No man loved laughing better, and his vein of humour was rich, and
apparently inexhaustible ... He would laugh at a stroke of genuine
humour, or sudden sally of odd absurdity, as heartily and freely as I
ever yet saw any man; and though the jest was often such as few
felt besides himself, yet his laugh was irresistible, and was observed
immediately to produce that of the company, not merely from the
notion that is was proper to laugh when he did, but purely out of
the want of the power to forbear it. (*JM* I, 269, 345)

These sentiments in Johnson suggest great purity of heart,
such as were those he responded to in Falstaff, of whom he
says: 'Yet the man thus corrupt, thus despicable, makes himself necessary to the prince that despises him, by the most
pleasing of all qualities, perpetual gaity, by an unfailing power
of exciting laughter' (*Johnson on Shakespeare* 523). Falstaff's
humour sounds like Johnson's, but, as Hawkins notes (a sentiment echoed by Boswell himself), in contradistinction to the
Falstaffian humour, 'Gesticular mimickry and buffoonery
[Johnson] hated' (164). True as this is, Johnson even indulged
in mimicry on occasions, as when, in Scotland, he imitates the
hopping of a kangaroo, or impersonates Lady Macdonald's
insipidity (the first episode not recounted by Boswell either in
the *Tour* or the *Life*). But 'gesticular mimickry' (the only
category of humour in which Mrs Thrale thought Johnson
deficient – see W. J. Bate, *Samuel Johnson* (London, 1978),
chapter 27) was precisely Boswell's forte (Mrs Thrale thought
he excelled in this). Mimicry, of course, is Boswell's metaphor
for his sympathetic relation to Johnson in the *Life* and is
intrinsic to his biographical method. It is no wonder that he
took every opportunity of doing down both Mrs Thrale and
Hawkins as serious biographers of Johnson.

Intrinsic to these shortcomings, however, is Boswell's complex sensitivity as biographer, as we see when we return to the
episode in which Johnson laughs at Langton's will-making.
When we compare the journal entry for 10 May 1773 in *Boswell
for the Defence* with the version in the *Life*, we notice the
same distancing in the latter already remarked on in Boswell's

'translating' from journal to *Life*. The *Life* registers a clearer note of disapprobation, adds the quality of veneration of Johnson (to accompany the awfulness and melancholy mentioned in both versions), and, surprisingly, removes Boswell's part in the fun. In the journal Boswell describes his response to Johnson's laughter: 'I cherished it, calling out, "Langton the testator, Langton Longshanks." This tickled his fancy so much that he roared out, "I wonder to whom he'll leave his legs?" ' (188). (Perhaps Johnson was so 'tickled' here because Boswell seems not to understand his use of 'testator', and merely mimicks Johnson's speech.) In addition, while the journal describes Johnson as 'full of drollery' and as participating in a 'most ludicrous scene' (188, 189), the *Life* has him giving a 'most ludicrous exhibition' and 'exulting in his own pleasantry' (549, 548). These are more than linguistic differences; 'exhibition' implies an act, as if Johnson's behaviour were not quite authentic, yet nonetheless private, beyond Boswell. Johnson's inaccessibility is reinforced by the idea of his 'exulting in his *own* pleasantry'. These differences might indicate, on a minute scale, the increased distance Boswell felt between himself and Johnson when looking back upon 1773 from 1791. It may also indicate a process of maturation. Even though the event of 1773 was incomprehensible, it was a 'scene' constituted by Boswell's imagination and his gaze, but also one in which he participated in the act of journal-writing, if not in actuality. By 1791 Johnson's inaccessibility was confirmed by his death, a difference that Boswell cannot assimilate, but which his prose registers. The version in the *Life* has a cadence never quite articulated, a shadow never quite focused.

Boswell's prose also registers some essence of Johnson's laughter without the cognitive recognition that he sought; paradoxically, he does this by discovering a purely private meaning in the laughter. The scene closes with the following:

This most ludicrous exhibition of the aweful, melancholy, and venerable Johnson, happened well to counteract the feelings of sadness which I used to experience when parting with him for a considerable time. I accompanied him to his door, where he gave me his blessing. (549)

As so often between the two men, the sadness at parting brings with it intimations and fears of a final parting, the loneliness of separation and of the individuation for which Boswell strives with Johnson, characteristic of Boswell's emotional life, inscribed into the act of writing Johnson's life. And here is Johnson's laughter, aimed so as to loosen our powerlessness in life, doing its work on Boswell by counteracting his feelings of sadness at parting from Johnson. Boswell's prose registers the sadness, perspicuously, unemotionally; he does not say that the feelings are not there, but that Johnson's laughter, mysteriously, makes them more bearable. This is a moment in which self-articulation and biographical recreation coincide.

Biography as seduction and appropriation: the Wilkes episode

The process of appropriation and self-definition I have been discussing is as ubiquitous as Boswell's consciousness. It is evident in particular scenes and encounters, as well as in the overall structure of the work. It is active in the meaning Boswell discovers and makes out of Johnson's attitudes to death, social hierarchy, and political allegiance, and also in his reading of Johnson's works. It is especially present in the final portrait of Johnson's character. Rader notes that 'Boswell's image of Johnson is the selective, constructive and controlling principle of the *Life*, the omnipresent element that vivifies and is made vivid in the whole' (29). Central to that image of Johnson is the conflict between body and spirit, and the transcendence of historical, material existence by moral judgement and intellectual activity. This grand dialectic comes to a head in the final character of Johnson, which will be more fully discussed below. But from the beginning of the work Boswell establishes Johnson as a man of powerful and eccentric bodily presence, and of unpredictable and potentially violent temper, and then subsumes those characteristics in a revelation of Johnson's kindness and humanity. In the episode of 26 October 1769, on the fear of death, discussed above (pp. 53–6), the harshness that Boswell experiences in Johnson's passion is finally resolved 'as one of the many proofs which his friends had, that though he might be charged with *bad humour* at times, he was always a *good-natured* man ... when upon any occasion Johnson had been rough to any person in company, he took the first opportunity of reconciliation, by drinking to him, or addressing his discourse to him' (429). And it was not only kindness that Boswell perceived as essential to Johnson, but also politeness: 'let it [not] be supposed that he was in a perpetual rage, and never without a club in his hand ... the truth is, that by much the greatest part of his time he was civil, obliging, nay, polite in the true sense of the word; so much so, that many gentlemen, who were long acquainted with him, never received, or even heard a strong expression from him' (777).

At the same time, having an idea of Johnson in accordance with the implied desire to fashion and authenticate a self through writing, and the other shaping principles of Boswell's biography mentioned above, carries with it a suggestion of Boswell's manipulation, and hence an indifference to certain levels of thought and experience in Johnson which, to other readers and biographers, are central to who Johnson is. Boswell's interlinked strengths and weaknesses are exemplified in the famous scene of Johnson's meeting with John Wilkes (1727–97) in May 1776. By 1776 Wilkes had a reputation as a rake and a radical political opportunist. Like Boswell, he was a lapsed Presbyterian; he had founded the Hell Fire Club and (with Charles Churchill) ran a journal called *The North Briton* that attacked government policy and King George III's Scottish favourites (especially the Earl of Bute). Between 1763 and 1768 Wilkes had gone into voluntary exile in France and Italy (where he had first met Boswell) after being prosecuted for seditious libel. After returning to England, Wilkes became member of Parliament for Middlesex in March 1768, but he was a wanted man, and was imprisoned after surrendering to the court in April. This began a series of expulsions from Parliament and re-elections by the Middlesex constituency that turned Wilkes into a national and international hero, who championed individual rights against ministerial abuse of power. Johnson refused to be impressed by Wilkes's behaviour during this period and treated him and his political arguments dismissively in 'The False Alarm' (1770). After release from prison in April 1770, Wilkes went into London politics where he fought to have parliamentary debates freely reported. In 1774 he was elected Mayor of London, and in the same year was again elected MP for Middlesex, and joined a small, ineffectual and relatively respectable radical faction in Parliament.

Johnson regarded Wilkes as a pernicious influence in public life, and would not willingly associate with him. When Boswell decides to bring the two men together he proposes a task that will test his social skills to the limit as well as his artistic skill as a biographer. The scene (764–76), in fact, is an epitome of the whole biography, and is an example of Boswell's comic and 'fictionalising' skill and ability to persuade us to see exactly the image of Johnson he wishes to convey. It is worth analysing in detail.

There are four parts of the episode on which I wish to concentrate (though not necessarily in this order): (1) the invitation to dinner and the potential obstacles to Johnson being there; (2) the initial scene in Dilly's drawing room in which Johnson sees Wilkes and Arthur Lee, the future American ambassador, and a 'patriot'; (3) the dinner; and (4) the conversation, including the final resolution between Johnson and Wilkes in an act of polite good humour.

By this point in the *Life* Johnson is secure in the reader's (and Boswell's) affection and admiration, and one of the functions of the episode is to qualify and enlarge our appreciation of Johnson by testing his character under circumstances in which he would normally react aggressively and anti-socially. The question Boswell poses to himself and to the reader is whether Johnson, given his temper and his firm religious and political principles, can subordinate himself in an act of sophisticated social goodwill by meeting Wilkes on affable terms. Boswell 'knows' that no ordinary invitation will reconcile Johnson to the prospect of socialising with Wilkes, so he devises a trick to have Johnson present. However, underlying this interest in enlarging Johnson's character, is a series of other, personal motives in Boswell's behaviour of which it is important the reader be aware.

The first reason Boswell offers for wishing to dramatise an occurrence that will 'with the liberal-minded, be much to [Johnson's] credit' (764) is his, Boswell's, 'desire of being much acquainted with celebrated men of every description'. He had socialised with Wilkes in Paris and Naples in 1765 and subsequently in London, and by 1776 he had known Johnson well for thirteen years. Typically Boswell felt that Johnson and Wilkes represented different sides of himself; he believed not only that he could 'fully relish the excellence of each', but that his 'delight in that intellectual chymistry, which can separate good qualities from evil in the same person', meant that he could bring them together (764). But the ideological differences between the two men seemed to preclude any possibility of their meeting amicably. 'Managing' the meeting is an irresistible challenge to Boswell (765). It is also a substitute for a different kind of meeting Boswell would like to witness: that between Johnson and Sir John Pringle, an old Scots Whig friend of Lord Auchinleck and Boswell ('mine own friend and my Father's friend', 764), between whom there was a mutual antagonism.

In other words, the opening of the Wilkes scene clearly shows that the affair was about Boswell's personal preoccupations as much as Johnson's character. Once Dilly has invited Boswell to dinner, and been persuaded by Boswell to include Johnson in the invitation, Boswell gets to work on Johnson. He does so by recognising Johnson's propensity to 'contradiction', and using it subtly to challenge Johnson's independence and his understanding as a social man:

While we were sitting quietly by ourselves at his house in an evening, [I] took occasion to open my plan thus: − 'Mr Dilly, Sir, sends his respectful compliments to you, and would be happy if you would do him the honour to dine with him on Wednesday next along with me, as I must soon go to Scotland.' JOHNSON. 'Sir, I am obliged to Mr Dilly. I will wait upon him −' BOSWELL. 'Provided, Sir, I suppose, that the company which he is to have, is agreeable to you.' JOHNSON. 'What do you mean, Sir? What do you take me for? Do you think I am so ignorant of the world, as to imagine that I am to prescribe to a gentleman what company he is to have at his table? BOSWELL. 'I beg your pardon, Sir, for wishing to prevent you from meeting people whom you might not like. Perhaps he may have some of what he calls his *patriotick* friends with him.' JOHNSON. 'Well, sir, and what then? What care *I* for his *patriotick friends*? Poh!' BOSWELL. 'I should not be surprized to find Jack Wilkes there.' JOHNSON. 'And if Jack Wilkes should be there, what is that to *me*, Sir? My dear friend, let us have no more of this. I am sorry to be angry with you; but really it is treating me strangely to talk to me as if I could not meet any company whatever, occasionally.' (765–6)

With a sure novelistic touch Boswell creates the domestic environment that is more than mere background: it validates the intimacy between the two men, and substantiates their emotional exchange. Johnson here speaks a relatively more formal language than in the other passages of direct speech discussed above (this is the conventional Johnson of 'No, Sir ...'); yet Johnson's (and Boswell's) formality is realistically convincing, for Boswell captures the accents and inflections of real conversational interchange. The reader is present and feels the emotional fluctuation in Johnson's voice as he moves from incredulity ('What do you mean, Sir?') to prickly disdain ('What care *I* for his *patriotick friends*? Poh!') to sensitive but firm mollification ('I am sorry to be angry with you; but really...'). At the same time Boswell is able clearly to distinguish himself from the voice he creates for Johnson: he plays the role of the naive, solicitous participant turned narrator ('I should not be surprized to find Jack Wilkes there').

The passage is at once realistically immediate, and invites the reader's imaginative participation in this moment of eighteenth-century life; it is also aware of its own artifice, delicately and self-consciously about something *other* than itself. As Sven Molin argues, it is part of a self-conscious exercise in the genre of the eighteenth-century comedy of manners. The transition between realism and narrative comment is smooth, but deliberate: 'Thus', Boswell says, 'I secured him, and told Dilly that he would find [Johnson] very well pleased to be one of his guests on the appointed day' (766). Boswell's confidence is a reflection of his temperamental self-assurance in social situations, but it is also based on his knowledge of how these events will turn out – writing the *Life* retrospectively, and because he has control over the dramatic creation of the scene itself, he knows that Johnson will be 'very well pleased' at Dilly's. This is a point towards which the overall narrative works, but, as critics (e.g. Ralph Rader) have discussed, Boswell introduces obstacles (such as the possibility that Johnson might dine at home that night with Mrs Williams when he forgets about the invitation) in order to create suspense, so that the eventual unison between Johnson and Wilkes carries a greater emotional and intellectual release and enjoyment.

That Boswell has an *idea* of where Johnson has to go in this scene to create a certain impression is clear from the word 'secure' (766) used to signify his feeling in the passage quoted above. It suggests not only catching Johnson but catching him *for* something; it suggests the idea of achievement. Having circumvented Mrs Williams's possible truculence and possessiveness (767), Boswell gets Johnson into Dilly's living room, where he encounters precisely the people who will test his character:

When we entered Mr Dilly's drawing room, [Johnson] found himself in the midst of a company he did not know ... I observed him whispering to Mr Dilly, 'Who is that gentleman, Sir?' – 'Mr Arthur Lee.' – JOHNSON. 'Too, too, too,' (under his breath,) which was one of his habitual mutterings ... 'And who is the gentleman in lace?' – 'Mr Wilkes, Sir.' This information confounded him still more ...
(767–8)

This is a crucial moment in the scene, since it is on Johnson's response that the harmony of the evening depends, as does Boswell's reputation (since it was he who assured Dilly of Johnson's compliance). So Boswell imagines Johnson remembering their conversation and then 'resolutely set[ting] himself to behave quite as an easy man of the world' (768). This is sufficient to take them into dinner, where the topics of conversation include the comedy of Foote and Garrick, Garrick's liberality, biography, a disputed passage in Horace, Settle, and Scotland. Boswell gives us one of his most comic and finely etched dialogues in tracing Johnson's passage at the dinner table from reluctant politeness to conviviality:

No man eat more heartily than Johnson, or loved better what was nice and delicate. Mr Wilkes was very assiduous in helping him to some fine veal. 'Pray give me leave, Sir: – It is better here – A little of the brown – Some fat, Sir – A little of the stuffing – Some gravy – Let me have the pleasure of giving you some butter – Allow me to recommend a squeeze of this orange; or the lemon, perhaps, may have more zest.' – 'Sir, Sir, I am obliged to you, Sir,' cried Johnson, bowing, and turning his head to him with a look for some time of 'surly virtue,' but, in a short while, of complacency. (768)

This little scene is very funny because of the underlying sense that the great moralist is having his heart softened by way of his stomach. Johnson's physical needs and weaknesses are depicted as dissolving his pride and making him less aloof. Wilkes's language and pliancy convey great shrewdness and are also most decorous and self-effacing, according to standards of polite eighteenth-century manners. His behaviour verges on the unctuous without actually becoming so. According to the logic of the scene Johnson can only eat and be content.

It is during conversation at dinner that the grand *rapprochement* between Johnson and Wilkes takes place. Boswell shapes the narrative so that the textual (and, apparently, the actual) harmony between the two antagonists comes about by setting himself over against them in a sacrificial gesture. He shares a knowledge of Scotland with them that separates the three from the rest of the company. When the subject of Scotland arises and the interlocutors exercise their wit on criticising the Scots, Boswell reflects: 'Upon this topick [Johnson] and Mr Wilkes could perfectly assimilate; here was a bond of union between them, and I was conscious that as both of them had visited Caledonia, both were fully satisfied of the strange narrow ignorance of those who imagine that it is a land of famine' (774). Johnson's final acceptance of and participation in Wilkes's complacency and considerateness is, as Rader writes, made by Boswell to reveal 'the full-hearted triumph of a capaciously human soul whose prejudice is only a temporary defect of its large virtues' (42), as the following excerpt shows:

[BOSWELL] … a seizure of [a] person [for debt], before judgement is obtained [in Scotland], can take place only, if his creditor should swear that he is about to fly the country ... WILKES. 'That, I should think, may be safely sworn of all the Scotch nation.' JOHNSON. (to Mr Wilkes) You must know, Sir, I lately took my friend Boswell and shewed him genuine civilised life in an English provincial town. I turned him loose at Lichfield, my native city, that he might see for once real civility: for you know he lives among savages in Scotland, and among rakes in London.' WILKES. 'Except when he is with grave, sober, decent people like you and me.' JOHNSON. (smiling) 'And we ashamed of him.'   (775)

The warmth of this scene, and the mutual consciousness between Johnson and Wilkes of antagonism entertained and declined, is a triumph of Boswell's contrivance and his art. Both Wilkes and Johnson speak with their own inflection, while also making an effort to express some of the tone of the other: Wilkes's playful joke about all Scotsmen wishing to leave Scotland is a gesture towards Johnson's mythic dislike of Scotland; Johnson's addressing himself directly to Wilkes, and adopting a tone of hyperbole in his mock-chastisement of Boswell, creates intimacy between himself and Wilkes. As Rader points out, Johnson's association of Boswell with 'rakes in London' implicitly acknowledges and neutralises the antagonism he has felt towards Wilkes (who had a reputation as a rake in London). Wilkes's response ('Except when he is with grave, sober, decent people like you and me') comically recognises and declines the antagonism, by aligning himself with Johnson. Johnson's smiling accepts Wilkes's response, recognises the beauty of the moment and affirms the connection with Wilkes ('And we ashamed of him'). As Rader says, 'the single adjective, 'smiling', applied to Johnson is, of course, not just a piece of random vividness, but is crucially important to our full sense of the active benevolence with which Johnson reconciles himself to Wilkes's (42).

The pleasure which this reconciliation generates is, of course, directly related to Boswell's dramatic artifice. The generosity in Johnson that the episode brings out is tested once more before the close of the scene, when Wilkes jokes about the Attorney-General, and openly refers to his trial for libel (775). Johnson's silence in response to what on another occasion might have stimulated an angry riposte leads Boswell to

conclude that 'he was now, *indeed*, "a good-humoured fellow"',
taking us back to the opening of the whole episode, and
reminding us of the social 'test' that he had proposed for
Johnson, and that Johnson had now wonderfully satisfied.

Burke's later compliment to Boswell that his 'negociation'
in this episode surpassed everything in 'the whole history of
the *Corps Diplomatique*' (776) has been echoed by many
critics (see chapter 2), who have assumed that the dramatic
coherence and conviction of Boswell's art − and the pleasure
it gives − actually *defines* who Johnson is. It is a mark of
Boswell's skill that critics such as Rader and Siebenschuh treat
his prose rhetorically, yet always take his *attitudes*, and the
judgements of Johnson they imply, as given. For them, there
is no question that what Boswell sees as Johnson's awkward-
ness and prejudice in the episode are given facts, which need
to be accepted by the reader so that Boswell can depict Johnson
transcending his own small-mindedness. Of course, these 'facts'
are themselves the object of Boswell's perception, emotional
and psychological make-up, and choice − a situation modern
Boswellian criticism is prepared to accept theoretically, but
not in practice, when it entails having to apply to Boswell
standards other than his own artistic principles. Molin, for
example, blandly says that because Boswell's opening remarks
state that the episode will be to Johnson's credit, therefore he
'establishes the truth of his account' (320). This self-reflexivity
underlies a chronic reluctance to see Boswell in relation to
a Johnson who lies outside Boswell's text − that is, to some
independent idea of how Johnson's mind works (such as
other biographies or Johnson's own works) − even when it is
claimed that Boswell's prose is being true to an independent,
historical Johnson. But Boswellian criticism's claim is a
double-edged sword: Boswell is taken as an accurate guide
to what Johnson is actually like, but this also means that we
are unable to give a really convincing account of Boswell's
book. So because Boswell conceives of Johnson's opposition
to Wilkes's politics and person only as a kind of eccentric
prejudice to be spirited away by an ingenious trick, the reader
is expected to enquire no further into the moral meaning of the

episode, and therefore into the really important relationship between the biographer and his subject.

One aspect of the moral meaning of the episode is located in Boswell's cleverness, presented to the reader in detail. If what Boswell tells us about Johnson is going to carry weight, his conduct as an active participant in the scene will have to bear the same moral scrutiny as one friend's behaviour towards another. No matter how generously Johnson is finally depicted as behaving, Boswell has nevertheless portrayed him as being manipulated and deceived, as being smaller than Boswell's understanding of his own nature and the situation as a whole. Some readers might not enjoy seeing Johnson cut down to size, but his limitation is not the issue I am discussing here (though Johnson's 'limitations' are integral to who he is, and thus important to a biographer). The point is about the relationship between Boswell and Johnson — a relationship that is central to Boswell's consciousness, whether one considers the scene as art or as life. Boswell's subordination of the means to the end, his deceit and manipulation (albeit benevolent) are at odds with friendship; moreover, they make Boswell the centre of attention (in his consciousness and ours), even though it is Johnson at whom we are smiling.

Another aspect of the moral meaning of the episode is the dramatic pleasure it conveys. Rader talks of the comic pleasure of the scene, and argues that our admiration for Johnson is proportionate to the pleasure experienced (37, 42). How generous and expansive is the pleasure we feel? My sense is that the pleasure of Boswell's scene is strictly circumscribed and controlled. The narrator's consciousness is so clearly defined and so separate from the participants in the action as well as from the reader, that the reader is rendered a passive spectator — he or she watches a play comparable in its intellectual wit to the Restoration and Georgian comedies that Boswell admired, rather than to drama of general nature in which, as Johnson says of Shakespeare, 'reflection strikes the heart' ('Preface' 78).

Once we feel the relative smallness of the dramatic pleasure *within* Boswell's scheme, we see that Boswell constructs an image of a man towards whom he is at once reverent *and* controlling:

I am now to record a very curious incident ... which I am persuaded will, with the liberal-minded, be much to his [Johnson's] credit ... They [Johnson and Wilkes] had even attacked one another with some asperity in their writings; yet I lived in habits of friendship with both. I could fully relish the excellence of each; for I have ever delighted in that intellectual chymistry, which can separate good qualities from evil in the same person ... Notwithstanding the high veneration which I entertained for Dr Johnson, I was sensible that he was sometimes a little actuated by the spirit of contradiction ...   (764—5)

This opening of the episode places Boswell's self at the centre of a fantasy encompassing the libertine and the moralist, in a similar way to his trying to reconcile the ideals of Erskine and Macdonald within himself in the *London Journal* (see above, pp. 12–14). Certainly he believes he knows Wilkes and Johnson better than they know themselves ('I could fully relish the excellence of each'). But Boswell's self-consciousness and his shaping presence in this scene — even when he subordinates himself as narrator — keep the action at a distance from the reader. The figure of Johnson in the scene is constrained by a kind of determining power outside his own volition, con- stituting, perhaps, a literary reflection of the theological pre- determination that Boswell felt in his life, and in response to which his social intercourse (both his libertinism and his exaggerated respect for hierarchy) was shaped. For Boswell, God's omniscience implied predestination, and while this prospect both comforted and terrified him (it guaranteed God's presence, but also God's judgement), he appeared to have felt no appreciation of the theological paradox involved in believing, as Johnson did, that while God was omniscient the will was still free, and that the first might be a guarantee of the second. Of Johnson's reluctance to attempt to untangle that paradox, Boswell makes one of his more crass remarks: 'he ... shrunk from an abridgement of an attribute usually ascribed to the Divinity, however irreconcileable in its full extent with the grand system of moral government. His sup- posed orthodoxy here cramped the vigorous powers of his understanding' (425, also 424). The disconnectedness of mind and heart that permits Boswell confidently to tackle the question of free will and predestination is reflected in his prose in general and in the Wilkes scene in particular: Johnson is not permitted to initiate the comedy; he can only be its object. The comedy therefore cannot be an expression of Johnson's freedom, but only of his place in Boswell's world.

Shakespeare's Falstaff (and Johnson's response to the character) is, once again, a good comparison by which to focus on that aspect of Johnson which is omitted from Boswell's picture. The scenes in *Henry IV*, Part I, in which Falstaff's cowardice and bravado are detected, and in which he and Hal take turns to impersonate the King (II.iv, 113–485) − scenes which Johnson thought 'supremely comic' ('Shakespeare' 472) − reveal the good humour Johnson found Falstaff to epitomise. In *Rambler* 72 Johnson calls good humour 'a habit of being pleased', or 'the act or emanation of a mind at leisure to regard the gratification of another' (II, 13). It can usually be called into being only by those who do not explicitly claim our admiration and so, confessing or revealing their foolish humanity, make it possible for us to forgo the assertion of our individuality or specialness. As Johnson says in *Rambler* 72 (II, 15), 'We are most inclined to love when we have nothing to fear.' It is Falstaff's good humour that potentiates the apparently contradictory responses Johnson has to him: 'Thou compound of sense and vice ...' ('Shakespeare' 523). Johnson's response to Falstaff is a kind of self-knowledge; Falstaff's weakness tells us something about ourselves, and the pleasure we feel in that recognition transcends our potential superiority (see Parker 47–51). Our sense of separateness *and* solidarity with a character who combines such different qualities as Falstaff, such despicable and such lovable qualities, is a mark of the expansion and relaxation of self that Shakespeare's drama occasions, and that Johnson answers in the pleasure of his passage on Falstaff, and when he writes of Shakespeare generally that 'Nothing can please many and please long, but just representations of general nature... the pleasures of sudden wonder are soon exhausted, and the mind can only repose on the stability of truth' ('Preface' 61–2).

Johnson is a man for whom we do not commonly feel the contempt that Falstaff arouses (though is there not a hint of contemptuousness mingled with Boswell's predatoriness? – 'I exulted as much as a fortune-hunter who has got an heiress into a post-chaise with him to set out for Gretna-Green' (767)). Boswell's depiction of Johnson with Wilkes, however, gives us none of the density and complexity of feeling, or the resulting pleasure, or love – and, therefore, none of the self-discovery and self-acceptance – that Johnson finds and exhibits in writing about Falstaff. The pleasure of Falstaff is the pleasure of being in general nature. How much love do we feel for Johnson when depicted in the midst of his embarrassment at being caught out? We may compare Falstaff with Boswell's Johnson:

Prince. What trick, what device, what starting hole canst thou now find out to hide thee from this open and apparent shame?
Poins. Come, let's hear, Jack. What trick has thou now?
Falstaff. By the Lord, I knew ye as well as he that made ye. Why, hear you, masters. Was it for me to kill the heir apparent?
(II.iv, 263–70)

When we entered Mr Dilly's drawing room, he [Johnson] found himself in the midst of a company he did not know. I kept myself snug and silent, watching how he would conduct himself. I observed him whispering to Mr Dilly, 'Who is that gentleman, Sir?' – 'Mr Arthur Lee.' – JOHNSON. 'Too, too, too,' (under his breath,) which was one of his habitual mutterings … 'And who is the gentleman in lace?' – 'Mr Wilkes, Sir.' This information confounded him still more; he had some difficulty to restrain himself, and taking up a book, sat down upon a window-seat and read, or at least kept his eye upon it intently for some time, till he composed himself. His feelings, I dare say, were aukward enough. But he no doubt recollected his having rated me for supposing that he could be at all disconcerted by any company, and he, therefore, resolutely set himself to behave quite as an easy man of the world.   (767–8)

Boswell's scene (already discussed above) is exquisitely imagined and depicted with precise dramatic conviction: it is difficult to doubt that this is what actually happened and that this is what Johnson thought and felt at Edward Dilly's home in 1776. But the reader who sees only the self-referential comic, artistic 'pleasure' underlying Johnson's transcendence of his limitations – in Boswell's terminology, Johnson becoming 'an easy man of the world' – has swallowed Boswell's rhetoric whole. The extent to which Boswell controls the scene is striking – not just artistically, in the sense of making choices of language, imagery, and pacing (as, indeed, he must as a biographer), but in the sense of controlling the reader's response, and his imagined Johnson. He has no hesitation in entering Johnson's mind to tell us what Johnson thinks and feels, to tell us what he 'would have thought' on this occasion. Yet this has the curious effect of objectifying Johnson, for all the key descriptive words, when considered as part of an interchange between one person and another, are intrusive and reflect how Johnson *is seen*, not necessarily how he felt on that historical occasion: 'confounded ... difficulty to restrain himself ... his feelings were aukward ... he no doubt recollected ... he resolutely set himself to behave ...' Under this apparent concern Johnson is objectified, the way women have been traditionally, and in the way Boswell treats Louisa in the *London Journal* (see above, pp. 23–7). As with Boswell's relation to Louisa and other women, he imagines himself setting the agenda: the passage under consideration assumes that Johnson's actions and feelings are motivated by Boswell and what passed between Boswell and Johnson ('he no doubt recollected his having rated me ...'). This could, of course, be pure fantasy and self-importance on Boswell's part; it is also an artistic means of psychologically encountering and defusing a threatening power and independence. With respect to women, that threat to Boswell is sexual and, because it involves control and ways of envisaging and recording reality textually, it is also political. In this sense both sexual and political issues are involved in Boswell's extraordinary depreciation of Mrs Thrale's *Anecdotes of Samuel Johnson*. He asserts his social superiority over Henry Thrale (1728–81), her husband (who is actually a very successful, rich brewer, Johnson's close friend, and a Member of Parliament – a position to which Boswell aspired). Then he enlists Johnson's words to disempower Mrs Thrale's literary achievements by subordinating her to her husband's authority: 'I know no man ... who is more master of his wife and family than Thrale ... It is a great mistake to suppose that she is above him in literary attainments' (349, and 347–8). Insofar as Boswell responds deeply and fundamentally to Johnson, so too does the threat of Johnson's independence touch Boswell's sexuality and political vision.

There is an impotence in the Wilkes episode associated with Boswell's detachment: he observes rather than participates actively, in ways that are not adequately explained by his position as narrator – 'I kept myself snug and silent, watching how he would conduct himself.' Boswell's excitement and the sense of power he derives from *watching* Johnson's difficulties is voyeuristic. This voyeuristic self-empowerment is at one with the disempowering of Johnson effected by virtue of Johnson's place in Boswell's consciousness (see above, p. 69). Psychoanalysis and film theory tell us that voyeuristic self-empowerment and excitement is derived from a created distance between the subject and an absent, irrecoverable object (see D. N. Rodowick, *The Difficulty of Difference* (London, 1991), chapter 2). At the same time, Boswell's apparent conviction that Johnson's difficulties are evidence of his own effectiveness is illuminated by Laura Mulvey's point that 'voyeurism ... has associations with sadism; pleasure lies in ascertaining guilt (immediately associated with castration), ascertaining control and subjecting the guilty person through punishment and forgiveness' (in Rodowick 5). Boswell may want Johnson to 'behave quite as an easy man of the world', exhibiting genuine politeness. He wants Wilkes and Johnson to be reconciled – 'it would have been much to be regretted if they had been for ever at a distance from each other' (776) – and to be like himself. But the unacknowledged, artistically sublimated propensity to control events, and the image of Johnson, is rooted in Boswell's psyche and sexuality. It suggests why Boswell misses other, Falstaffian dimensions of Johnson's good humour. In the words of *Rambler* 72 (on good humour), Boswell's 'mind is not at leisure to regard the gratification of another'. His own gratification is uppermost because his own *idea* of Johnson is so important to him. In *Rambler* 72

Johnson says, 'we are most inclined to love when we have nothing to fear'. The voyeuristic sense of power Boswell generates in the Wilkes scene is founded on fear; the punishment and forgiveness are the grounds on which Johnson's otherness and power are (in Boswell's experience) de-activated and acceptable.

Rambler 72 points out that the need to admire another destroys good humour, and imprisons one within the individual self. The art of the *Life* (including the Wilkes scene under discussion) is a reflection both of Boswell's attempt to break out of that circle of self and of the means by which he remains where he is. Through manipulation Boswell seeks security psychologically re-enacting a Calvinistic predetermination; but his activity rebounds destructively because the Johnson of his creation cannot break through the mediacy of his fictional-ising. This disappointment produces no explicit guilt – nor does the voyeuristic depletion of Johnson's power – as do other eighteenth-century Calvinist-influenced works, such as William Godwin's *Caleb Williams* (1794). But there is, as I have been arguing, a frozen, unengaged quality to the artistic perfection, reflected not least in the fact that Johnson and Wilkes are not *really* reconciled in principle and philosophy, despite the incredible politeness and momentary intimacy they share with each other on a second dinner engagement in 1781 (which, presumably, would not have happened had Boswell not 'negotiated' the first). (On the second date Boswell notes: 'I was struck with observing Dr Samuel Johnson and John Wilkes, Esq., literally *tête-à-tête*; for they were reclined upon their chairs, with their heads leaning almost close to each other, and talking earnestly, in a kind of confidential whisper' (1147).)

If Boswell's manipulation and assimilation of Johnson in the main Wilkes episode is a means of acknowledging Johnson's power and disempowering him at the same moment, then his relationship with Johnson (or his fictional Johnson) in this scene is also a playing out of the psychological double bind that he experienced as the object of his father's abusive and indifferent power, and which he has internalised (see above, pp. 17–20). Lord Auchinleck's power divides Boswell; reconciling

Johnson with Wilkes is an artistic means of neutralising the anxiety generated by inexplicable and indifferent power. The shadow of the indifferent and mysteriously obscure deity of Calvinism (see Manning, *Puritan–Provincial Vision* 9–10) lurks within Boswell's biographical image of Johnson, and is directly connected to Boswell's repeated attempts to persuade Johnson to pontificate definitively on theologically and experientially inexplicable matters, such as the nature of the afterlife. Writing of the anxiety brought about by the fear of a future which we cannot *certainly* know to be bad, Johnson remarks that 'anxiety of this kind is nearly of the same nature with jealousy in love' (*Rambler* 29, I, 160).

Boswell's reverence for and idealisation of Johnson is rooted in a need to be loved and accepted by his father, and to create a 'supporting, imaginary father' (Kristeva, p. 17 above) who guarantees self-empowerment and articulation. To the extent that Boswell casts Johnson in this role, he shrinks from directly challenging Johnson's authority. Only once in the *Life* (2 May 1778) does Boswell express his anger at the aggressive rudeness with which Johnson sometimes attacked him. But Boswell does not express or acknowledge the anger *to Johnson*. The hurt Boswell really feels prompts him to absent himself from Johnson's presence, but, as with his response to Louisa, this is a way of punishing Johnson: 'I was so much hurt, and had my pride so much roused, that I kept away from him for a week; and, perhaps, might have kept away much longer, nay, gone to Scotland without seeing him again, had not we fortunately met and been reconciled' (983). By the time they effect a reconciliation, on 8 May, the emotional hurt that Boswell feels (and any person might naturally feel at Johnson's rudeness) has become 'unease' at being treated unkindly 'before people who neither love you nor me': 'it gave those persons [not of the Johnsonian school] an opportunity of enlarging upon his supposed ferocity, and ill treatment of his best friends'. The direct emotional interchange between Johnson and Boswell has become a spectacle at which Boswell watches himself violated before other people — a psychological and emotional double consciousness indicative of much of his prose. I suggest that the anger that Boswell feels at having his self-esteem gratuitously violated cannot be directly expressed to Johnson because that would threaten his sense of self by representing a violation of the object of his veneration; it questions the ideal with which he has invested Johnson, and therefore undermines the potency of the 'supportive, imaginary father' that is the object of his art. Expressing his anger at Johnson would mean acknowledging that the particular love that Boswell seeks from him could only be had from himself and from his grounding in God and the world. Indeed, it would betoken his having *already* realised the love he seeks. (On this occasion, Johnson does not help, but falls into Boswell's scheme by pampering him: 'Well, I am sorry for it. I'll make it up to you twenty different ways, as you please' (983).)

In making his portrait of Johnson, and playing himself off against this man invested with all Boswell's ideals, the biographer is trying to articulate himself, to make meaningful a life too often given to fictionalising and role-playing. In other words, in the absence of the love of God and of the father, he is trying to love himself. It is ironic therefore that the effort to keep Johnson present in biography, via memory, as a guarantor of Boswell's own empowerment is, as I have been discussing, conducted in a prose that undercuts its deepest aims. It is a prose that encourages an inwardness and illusion of self-sufficiency, and (unlike Johnson's *Rambler* style) builds into itself a clarity and privacy that closes it to falsification, and therefore to confirmation, subtly evading not only the challenge to its propositions but even the thought of challenge. Hence the uniform praise of Boswell's artifice by modern critics.

All of the immediately above makes Boswell very Humean, yet without Hume's intellectual penetration, or his sceptical poise. It also makes Boswell very modern in his sensibility, for the *Life* is deeply concerned with and manifests the aporia of language that has come to be seen by modern criticism as an intelligent response to a fragmentary and secular world.

Chapter 5

The ending of the *Life* and the meaning of Johnson's character

The character of Johnson created in the *Life*, through the scenes, the accumulated conversations and details, and through Boswell's response to Johnson within the imaginative world of the book, is of a multi-faceted, multi-layered hero. The *Life* is compared to the *Odyssey* in the advertisement to the second edition (1793), but unlike Odysseus or Ulysses – whose journeys are of political and dynastic discovery – Johnson's is that of the exemplary Christian hero, of one who has undergone and faced the challenges and temptations of his own passions and fears, and through the 'power of virtue and of wisdom' (7) has arrived at a place where he is reconciled to God. The *Life* is a secular *Pilgrim's Progress*.

Throughout the work there is a tension between the goodness and piety that characterise Johnson's actions and attitudes to others, and the struggle within Johnson that prevents him from accepting Providential grace. The reconciliation of these two sides manifests itself in particular scenes (such as the Wilkes scene) and is also elaborately traced by Boswell in the account of Johnson's last days and the exemplary way in which he comports himself on his death-bed. Dowling notes that the dramatic context of Johnson's death as a Christian hero summarises his inward struggle through the *Life* as a whole; the story of that struggle prepares us for Boswell's account of Johnson's end as a Christian hero who passes through doubt and repentance to tranquillity (*Boswellian Hero* 172). At the same time Johnson's exemplary Christianity is indivisible from the powerful effect of his presence upon Boswell and, indeed, upon the world in which Boswell places him. For Boswell, Johnson's heroism transforms and glorifies a mundane world even while he, Johnson, remains separate and above that world. While Johnson's life is symbolic of his orthodox

Anglicanism and Toryism, the significance associated with his particular, authoritative presence is the result of Boswell's biographical and dramatic fictionalising. According to Boswell's logic, Johnson's presence-as-phenomenon – the particular spiritual significance of his character – is accessible only through the recreative process represented by the *Life of Johnson*. Johnson comes for Boswell to be *the* example of authentic personal presence and expressiveness, maintaining the belief in a heroic capacity to break through the mediacy and contingency of one's own life in history (Bogel, 'Johnson Plain' 77–8). Because Boswell presents Johnson as being *in fact* like this when he is creating an image of Johnson in language, Johnson's 'presence' acutely throws up the question of the relation between truth, historical existence, and writing.

Discovering a heroic significance in Johnson's life does not preclude criticism of Johnson. It is one of Boswell's strengths that he countenances disagreements with Johnson (they disagreed on American independence, slavery, legal entails on property, Hume, Rousseau, sexual promiscuity, the poetry of Gray and Mason, Ossian and Scottish culture, and many other things). The coexistence of admiration and disagreement is made possible by Boswell's distinguishing between the natural man in Johnson – his mundane, temporal, historical life, subject to temper, passion, and therefore to misconceptions – and the moral essence that his portrait aims to elicit, the triumph of which underpins Boswell's claim to Johnson's heroism. The distinction between Johnson's historical existence and his essence, between nature and spirit in the *Life* is compellingly put by Rader: 'Boswell's book ... lifts an aspect of human reality from the contingency of history and displays it as a concrete universal – self-validating, self-intelligible, inherently moving, permanently valuable. For what we experience finally in the book ... is not the sum of Johnson's particular actions but the essence of his character, an essence deeply relevant not to the contingency of history but to the permanence of human nature and therefore immediately to ourselves' ('Literary Form' 48).

This universality of Boswell's art is fully displayed in his closing portrait of Johnson's character (1398–1402). The portrait opens with Boswell suggesting that the character of Johnson has been implicit and developed throughout the particulars of the book, because it 'has been so developed in the course of this work, that they who have honoured it [the work] with a perusal, may be considered as well acquainted with' Johnson (1398) as the author. To read Boswell's work is to 'read' and understand Johnson. Yet the structure and the content of this final portrait bring out some of Boswell's major preoccupations with a clarity not evident in the body of the book. It is significant that the portrait is adapted from the opening pages of the *Tour to the Hebrides*. In a note Boswell refers to their similarity: 'I do not see any reason to give a different character of my illustrious friend now' (1398). There are significant differences, however, between the two worth noting because they touch on Boswell's particular vision in the *Life*: on a general level the portrait in the *Life* is more exemplary and judgemental, as if Johnson now, in 1791, signified more than he did in 1786. The prose in the later work is more subtle, less stylistically simple – less polite and pure in an Addisonian sense – and aims to convey more information about Johnson, particularly by demonstrating the multiplicity and connectedness of his personal characteristics. While both portraits establish Johnson's religious and moral character as dominating all other attributes of his personality, his metaphysical and symbolic presence in the *Life* is complicated by a more substantial physical element.

In fact, the portrait in the *Life* early on refers to Johnson's appearance and physique, and returns at a number of points to details of this kind, while the portrait in the *Tour* retains these details till last, as merely one aspect of Johnson's existence in this life, along with all the others. The version in the *Life* opens as follows (with which the version in the *Tour* could be further compared than my analysis on pp. 33–7):

His figure was large and well formed, and his countenance of the cast of an ancient statue; yet his appearance was rendered strange and somewhat uncouth, by convulsive cramps ... So morbid was his temperament, that he never knew the natural joy of a free and vigorous use of his limbs: when he walked, it was like the struggling gait of one in fetters; when he rode, he had no command or direction of his horse, but was carried as if in a balloon. That with his constitution and habits of life he should have lived seventy-five years, is a proof that an inherent *vivida vis* [lively force] is a powerful preservative of the human frame.   (1398–9)

This descriptive passage moves through different stages towards a complex moral and intellectual evaluation of Johnson. It sets up a contact and qualifying contrast between mind and body in Johnson that structures the whole portrait. Johnson's physical being is noble and powerful, yet it is contorted. He is at once in the ancient world of Classical art untouched by life ('of the cast of an ancient statue'), and he is tormented by physical pain ('convulsive cramps'). The 'uncouthness' of his appearance becomes an image for Johnson's morbidity, a temperament that hinders a free interchange with the world on both the intellectual and physical plains: 'he never knew the natural joy of a free and vigorous use of his limbs: when he walked, it was like the struggling gait of one in fetters'. Yet, as the paragraph proceeds Boswell discovers a deeper paradox in Johnson's existence, for his temperament is subordinated to a greater spirit, energy of mind, that sustains the body against all the medical odds, yet in so doing makes it ludicrous ('he had no command of his horse ...'). The effect of this paradox is that Johnson's mind is not at home within his body, certainly not 'at one' with it; nor is his body at one with the world, for the exercise of mind took the form of a heroic struggle against great physical and natural restrictions: 'when he walked, it was like the struggling gait of one in fetters'. Boswell's long, meandering, but tightly structured paragraph traces a series of ascending discrepancies in Johnson between world and body, between body and mind, and between mind and spirit.

The dualism is then focused in a general statement about the nature of mind, and the relation between the realm of intellect and the realm of historical, social, and physical contingency:

Man is, in general, made up of contradictory qualities; and these will ever shew themselves in strange succession, where a consistency in appearance at least, if not in reality, has not been attained by long habits of philosophical discipline. In proportion to the native vigour of the mind, the contradictory qualities will be more prominent, and more difficult to be adjusted ...   (1399)

The first sentence of this quotation tries, perhaps, to sound like the opening statement of a *Rambler* essay; it is a general *sententia*, summarising a large experience, and offering itself for examination and elaboration. Johnson himself often strikes a similar note; for example:

The mind of man is never satisfied with the objects immediately before it, but is always breaking away from the present moment, and losing itself in schemes of future felicity ...   (*Rambler* 2, I, 9)

Boswell's general statement is subdivided into two subordinate alternatives − 'appearance' and 'reality' − subsumed under the notion of 'contradictory qualities', and closes in a new position that nonetheless echoes the finality of the opening. 'Long habits of philosophical discipline' is a given, it is where Boswell starts and ends. Johnson, on the other hand, sustains his thought through several paragraphs and, sometimes, several pages, developing, qualifying, expanding, opening, reinventing his initial thought to uncover one layer after another in the human mind and human experience. In the case of the opening proposition to *Rambler* 2 (above), the emptiness and vacancy of the mind turns out, in the course of the essay, to be the conditions for great self-knowledge and an intimate, spacious, feeling experience not given, but discovered.

But Boswell has difficulty *making* anything of the opening proposition: the idea of contradictory qualities is really no more than an idea about vacillation, and has a very personal resonance for Boswell himself. Johnson was a complex and tempestuous man, but he was not fickle. Boswell here finds the same difficulty in connecting up alternate perceptions as he had in encompassing the different sides of himself represented by Erskine and McDonald, discussed above (pp. 12−14, 71−2). However, he compensates for that division in the self −

expressed as a rhetorical split − by proposing an interesting explanation for the operation of the mind that goes to the heart of how he sees Johnson. Great powers of mind *magnify* contradictory qualities, and therefore place the possessor firmly against consistency, form, coherence, qualities which 'philosophical discipline' might be able to cultivate 'in appearance at least', but not in reality.

This idea reveals a dualism in Boswell's experience between the realm of mind and the realm of nature, that anticipates the idealism of Coleridge and the Schlegels, all of whom followed the transcendental philosophy of Kant and Schelling: 'Every fine painting comes into being through the removal of what one might call the invisible partition that separates the real from the ideal world; it is in itself no more than the gateway to the world of the imagination' (Schelling, quoted by Parker 78). For Boswell, coming from a Calvinist background stressing the fallen nature of humanity and the ineffectualness of the human will, nature is a realm providing little spiritual sustenance, and therefore mind translates theological contingencies into a secularity, and seeks compensation for life's imperfection, by transforming 'fallen' nature into an ideal. Boswell's idea, though not fully thought out, is not unlike Coleridge's notion of the transmuting power of imaginative art − the capacity of the imagination in great art to reconcile opposites (*Biographia Literaria*, chapter 14), supported by Kant's idea in the *Critique of Judgement*: 'The imagination ... is very powerful in creating what might be called a second nature out of the material given it by actual nature' (quoted by Parker 65). Parallel to this proto-idealism in Boswell's thinking about mind, is, as I have discussed earlier, an attitude to history and biography that sanctions the free use of artifice in order to create a complex image of Johnson in accordance with an inner *idea*, but which, at the same time, claims the status of fact and historical truth.

There is nothing theoretically problematic in this manoeuvre, but it does have practical difficulties for the way Boswell understands Johnson and actually reads his works. This process of thought permits Boswell to cite Johnson's 'limitations' and at the same time to subsume them within the heroic idea of

Johnson which the *Life* as a whole elaborates. Hence, Boswell
reasons, Johnson stood strongly by and defended his religious
and political principles, but he had 'narrowed his mind
somewhat too much, both as to religion and politicks'. Likewise, Johnson is both aware of the dangers of free thinking,
and very independent of spirit, and this conflict 'occasioned
his appearing somewhat unfavourable to the prevalence of
that noble freedom of sentiment which is the best possession
of man' (1399). Boswell countenances these annoying 'anomalies' because he believes that within the realm of Johnson's
heroism – that is, from the point of view of the nature
of mind suggested by Boswell's method – these contradictions (necessary contradictions incident to the 'native
vigour of the mind') are sublimated in the essence of Johnson's
mind and character. This is a different issue from the strength
of spirit Boswell admires when recording how Johnson fought
illness: 'there was in him an animated and lofty spirit, and
however complicated diseases might depress ordinary mortals,
all who saw him, beheld and acknowledged the *invictum
animum Catonis* [Cato's stubborn soul]' (1357). However,
it is necessary to acknowledge that in privileging the sub-
limating, redemptive qualities of mind over nature in an
account of Johnson's *thought*, Boswell is at odds with some
of Johnson's central intuitions and convictions about life and
art (and, in this precise form, anticipates many modern critics
of Johnson).

Boswell as critic of Johnson's works

Boswell's general interpretation of mind shapes his reading
of such major works of Johnson as the *Rambler* (1750–2),
the *Dictionary* (1755), *Rasselas* (1759) and *The Lives of the
Poets* (1779–81). This reading is absolutely central to a full-
scale biography of the greatest person of letters in the English
eighteenth century. Of course, no reader as attentive to detail
and as interested in Johnson as Boswell was is likely to be
a wholly misleading reader of Johnson's works; but it is
precisely to the extent that Boswell gives himself over to

Johnson as one of great personal importance to himself that he misreads Johnson's works.

Boswell's response to *Rasselas* is a case in point. *Rasselas* is a tale about growing up and coming to terms with the limits and opportunities of life. Prince Rasselas, his sister Nekayah, her maid Pekuah, and their philosopher-guide Imlac leave the utopian 'Happy Valley' to make a 'choice of life' out in the world. The story documents the disappointments experienced by the characters in their search for a perfect life, until, a little wiser and a little sadder, they return to the place from which they began. *Rasselas* is a deceptively simple tale. Not only does it satirise optimism but it also embodies complex truths about the nature of the human mind in its propensity to hope and idealise. The tale's apparently clear, confident moral arguments are constantly modified by Johnson's rhetoric and the larger sympathetic understanding of human action that comes with it. General moral arguments are constantly modified by particular incidents. Though individual characters (especially Imlac) speak with a 'Johnsonian' authority, Johnson is not finally identified with any of the characters – the tale as a whole (its narrative, structure, humorous-rueful tone, and penetrating human insights) is more than any particular idea it contains, and, indeed, more than the sum of its parts.

Boswell summarises *Rasselas* (240–4) as follows: the tale leads us through the most important scenes of life, and 'shews us that this stage of our being is full of "vanity and vexation of spirit"' (the quotation is from *Ecclesiastes* I, 14); to fully appreciate the tale one must accept that human nature has fallen from the state of its created perfection, and one must look beyond the present life; in our present state there is more evil than good (241). In other words, *Rasselas* is (as Boswell himself says, 242) a prose version of the *Vanity of Human Wishes*, enforcing a vision of the imperfect, unsatisfactory, fallen nature of human life, and necessitating the cultivation of a vision of a compensating, Christian afterlife. In order to distinguish Johnson from Voltaire's attack upon the philosophical doctrine of optimism and the sceptical treatment of Providence and revelation in *Candide* (also published in 1759), Boswell emphasises the element of Christian teleology in *Rasselas*: 'Johnson meant, by shewing the unsatisfactory nature of things temporal, to direct the hopes of man to things eternal' (242). Now, although Johnson and Voltaire are radically different in their attitude towards divinity, and although a Christian teleology might be extrapolated from *Rasselas*, Boswell's summary of the work is inadequate in other respects since it responds to only one of its elements. It is as if – like many modern readers who identify Johnson with Imlac – Boswell had identified Johnson and the entire book with Nekayah, who, after she and the other characters have experienced many disappointments in trying to choose a perfect way of living, free of compromises, remarks, 'To me ... the choice of life is become less important; I hope hereafter to think on the choice of eternity' (*Rasselas*, ed. D. J. Enright (Penguin, 1979), 149).

Nekayah's statement, however, represents only one point of view amongst several fictional characters within a comprehensive work. *Rasselas* deals with what is historical in human experience, rather than advocating a Providential view of history. Nekayah's words occur in the penultimate chapter, in which the characters discuss the nature of the soul; but unlike the entirely natural attempts on the part of the characters within the book to define the thing they discuss (the nature of the soul), the book itself reveals the nature of the soul through experience, through action and time, circumstantially, and through the dramatic interaction between characters. It does not formulate the nature of the soul doctrinally or intellectually. For Johnson knows that 'Human experience, which is constantly contradicting theory, is the great test of truth' (*Life* 319). So a dynamic interrelationship between the mind and the limits of life 'beyond' the mind informs both single episodes in *Rasselas* and the structure of the book as a whole. Imlac aphoristically catches the moral dilemma of mind in the midst of the process of living when he says to Rasselas and the other characters, 'It seems to me ... that while you are making the choice of life, you neglect to live' (103). The way Johnson handles that potential dualism, the opposition between mind and body, between spiritual and material realms, is what gives substance and spiritual meaning to the knowledge that the soul manifests itself in the present moment; and that moment, within the imaginative world of *Rasselas*, is the *only* reality on which to base moral action and choice.

This view implies a deep experiential tact and self-confidence – not only an acceptance, but an active incorporation of the imperfect nature of human understanding into the self – which Boswell has difficulty in comprehending. Unlike *Rasselas* (and Johnson's moral thought in general), that finds in given limitations of personality and the imperfect nature of human knowledge subjects for rejoicing and self-revelation, Boswell finds these realities troubling; they are experiences from which the present moment offers escape. So his interpretation of *Rasselas* fragments: having emphasised the melancholy of the book, having attributed to Johnson, on *this* basis, less enjoyment of life than he, Boswell, had, and then having turned back on himself to acknowledge that 'there is too much of reality in the gloomy picture' offered by Johnson, Boswell dissolves it all by saying, 'The truth, however, is, that we judge of the happiness and misery of life differently at different times, according to the state of our changeable frame' (243). But as usual, this apparent Montaigne-like, or Johnsonian, sceptical flexibility is not sustained beyond the text; there is no substance to the prose, it does not engage with life.

While 'truth' is certainly elusive for Johnson, and has everything to do with humankind's existential place, it nonetheless exists within the nexus of mind, body, and spirit; within the nexus of past, present, and future, and of the historical and the transcendent. Boswell feels more comfortable in connecting the elusiveness of truth, and the human uncertainties associated with it, with a Christian afterlife, with an absolute that removes uncertainties. Boswell is a little like the character Rasselas in that he wants to settle the question of living quickly and neatly, once and for all. But the conventional religious consolation to which Boswell seeks to tie

Rasselas is a mark of the absence of real religious consolation within his own soul. Because he needs the Christian element so much he emphasises its function, but thereby blurs what part it does play in Johnson's work, and how Johnson is able to blend religious and secular, spiritual and material elements in his thought. Boswell's inclination to read *Rasselas* as a tale of Christian consolation underlies his general portrait of Johnson's mind as one that sublimates the material and natural world into spirit.

Boswell reads *Rasselas* didactically, without registering Johnson's language, wit, and good humour. His critiques of the *Dictionary* (131–8, 209–15) and the *Rambler* (146–61) repeat this pattern. The stylistic principle in Johnson's prose that most impresses Boswell is what the eighteenth century called 'justness' of expression, the equal and adequate co-incidence of thought and word. Of the *Rambler* Boswell says:

By reading and meditation, and a very close inspection of life, he had accumulated a great fund of miscellaneous knowledge, which, by a peculiar promptitude of mind, was ever ready at his call, and which he had constantly accustomed himself to clothe in the most apt and energetick expression. (145)

As an observation on Johnson's intellectual seriousness and penetration, and the wisdom of such philosophical, humane expression, Boswell's words are an accurate tribute. But the question remains as to the nature of the 'most apt and energetick expression'. Boswell praises the Plan of the *Dictionary* for its freedom from stylistic inflation (133), and singles out the Preface for its 'clear, strong, and glowing style' and 'the perspicuity with which he has expressed abstract scientifick notions' (209). These are by no means inappropriate descriptions of Johnson's style in the *Dictionary*, yet Boswell is silent on Johnson's recognition of the historical, relative nature of language, and hence the difficulty people have in both writing and speaking so as to make words completely express ideas. This discrepancy between words and ideas, or, to put it another way, between language and the larger experience to which language can be put in literature, is a linguistic version of the discrepancy between optimistic ideas and actual human experience with which *Rasselas* deals, and which Boswell overlooked in his passages on the tale. In the *Dictionary* Johnson is aware that lexicography is paradoxical; the very idea of linguistic stability implied in the act of making a dictionary is undercut or qualified by his knowledge of the changeability of language:

This recommendation of steadiness and uniformity does not proceed from an opinion that particular combinations of letters have much influence on human happiness; or that the truth may not be success-fully taught by modes of spelling fanciful and erroneous: I am not yet so lost in lexicography as to forget that *words are the daughters of earth, and that things are the sons of heaven.* Language is only the instrument of science, and words are but the signs of ideas ...
(Preface to *Dictionary*, *Samuel Johnson*, ed. Donald Greene (Oxford, 1984), 310)

Boswell, however, writes about Johnson's prose as if sons and daughters were one. Johnson uses metaphor to bridge the gap between dictionary definitions of words and greater 'poetic' meanings which words can achieve. The *Dictionary* operates on the assumption that words and things, and thought and experience are not the same, and Johnson's explicit arguments about the nature of language, and his actual prose, attempt to accommodate those differences. Boswell, however, ignores Johnson's distinctions and tone. He sees Johnson's response to the irony of human history (as reflected in the history of the English language) in merely personal terms: 'we must ascribe its [the ending of the Preface] gloom to that miserable dejection of spirits to which he was constitutionally subject, and which was aggravated by the death of his wife two years before' (213). Boswell's tendency is to value what is fixed, that which is clearly delineated to the exclusion of change, and so it is natural that he judges the definitions in the *Dictionary* as 'astonishing proofs of acuteness of intellect and precision of language' and of 'a genius of the highest rank' (211). They certainly are a *tour de force*, but Johnson gives perhaps more weight in the Preface to the proposition that definitions by themselves are inadequate to understand

the nature and history of the English language; because
definitions cannot exhaust meaning, 'the solution of all difficulties, and the supply of all defects, must be sought in
the examples subjoined to the various sense of each word,
and ranged according to the time of their authors' (Preface
318). 'Examples' refers to the quotations from works of
literature and philosophy chosen by Johnson to illustrate
the broader range of 'meanings' that escape lexicographical
definition on an experiential level. The very process of defining
words is, for Johnson, connected to an appreciation of the
poetic and experiential content of language (a 'timelessness'),
but also to an understanding that the use (and therefore the
'meanings') of words changes over time (their 'historical'
character).

Boswell's response to Johnson's discussion of the nature
of language in the *Dictionary* simplifies and moralises the
process I have been discussing. He distinguishes the illustrative
quotations only for 'improvement and pleasure', and for
deliberate moral guidance: 'it should not pass unobserved,
that [Johnson] has quoted no author whose writings had a
tendency to hurt sound religion and morality' (136). His remarks
on the *Rambler* are also shaped by a moral purpose. Though
he remarks on Johnson's 'fund of miscellaneous knowledge'
(in the passage quoted above, p. 89), Boswell chooses to
emphasise the solemn 'character for which [Johnson] was
eminently qualified, a majestick teacher of moral and religious
wisdom'. This subject, Boswell thinks, invalidated the title
of 'Rambler' Johnson chose for his essays: 'Johnson was,
I think, not very happy in the choice of his title, *The Rambler*,
which certainly is not suited to a series of grave and moral
discourses' (143). But this is to underplay the flexibility of
thought and of language that characterises the *Rambler*, to
stereotype Johnson as a grave moralist when the essays (as
Philip Davis's *In Mind of Johnson* beautifully demonstrates)
reveal him as sceptical, Socratic, multi-faceted. Boswell's
difficulty in comprehending Johnson's flexibility in the *Rambler*
is brought out in the lengthy discussion of Johnson's prose
style (155–61).

The religious function of the *Rambler* for Boswell is clear: it 'has given a true representation of human existence, and ... has ... with a generous benevolence, displayed every consolation which our state affords us' (153). Nonetheless, when he comes to write of its style, he suggests (thereby echoing many contemporary critics and anticipating many modern ones) a division between the eloquence and the substance, the style and the ideas of Johnson's writing. Boswell's defence of Johnson's prose against those who accuse it of turgidness is that big ideas need big words – an idea expressed by Johnson himself (*Idler* 70, *Rambler* 168) – and, again, that 'Johnson's comprehension of mind was the mould for his language. Had his conceptions been narrower, his expression would have been easier. His sentences have a dignified march ...' (156, 158–9).

But it is clear that this style is not very congenial to Boswell, however much he may admire it. *The Tatler* (1709–10), the *Spectator* (1711–14), and the *Guardian* (1713) were the formative periodical essays in eighteenth-century England. Boswell compares Johnson's prose with Addison's, representative of an earlier, different cultural praxis. In comparison with Addison, Johnson is aloof and dictatorial; auditors 'attend with awe and admiration; and [Johnson's] precepts are impressed upon them by his commanding eloquence ... such is the melody of his periods, so much do they captivate the ear, and seize upon the attention, that there is scarcely any writer ... who does not aim ... at the same species of excellence' (160–1). Addison is more social, more flattering, more congenial, more human for Boswell: 'Addison writes with the ease of a gentleman. His readers fancy that a wise and accomplished companion is talking to them, so that he insinuates his sentiments and taste into their minds by an imperceptible influence ...' (160). And Boswell closes his enthusiastic description of Addison's prose by quoting Johnson's words on Addison's style from the 'Life of Addison':

What he attempted, he performed; he is *never feeble*, and he did not wish to be energetick; he is never rapid, and he never stagnates. His sentences have neither studied amplitude, nor affected brevity:

his periods, though not diligently rounded, are voluble and easy. Whoever wishes to attain an English style, familiar but not coarse, and elegant but not ostentatious, must give his days and nights to Addison.   (*Life* 161)

Not only is Addison's prose more polite and more congenial to Boswell, but Boswell's prose is more like Addison's than it is like Johnson's. Johnson's description of Addison's prose immediately above could equally well be applied to Boswell's passage on Johnson's *Rambler* style quoted on p. 89 above. Boswell has an Addisonian ease; phrases are effortlessly concatenated; words have no difficulty in dealing with large thoughts or experiences; the thought is of a great writer's style, but Boswell's prose registers no strain in tackling Johnson's style; the relationship between all the parts in Boswell's passage is effortless, social, polite. In other words, there is a certain depth and experiential richness in Johnson's prose not registered in Boswell's attempt to describe it. The ease of Boswell's passage is captured in the supple commonplace and the aphoristic jingle of Johnson's phraseology in his description of Addison's prose.

Boswell's prose fails to convey a sense of the integrity of Johnson's style – of how style shapes ideas, and vice versa; why, in fact, the suggestion of a separation of style and content in the *Rambler* is misleading for what happens in Johnson's writing and thinking. The comprehensiveness of mind to which Boswell refers in his critique appears, in Boswell's experience (rather than just in his terminology), to *exclude* much of the experiential substantiality, the embodiment of general truths in particular instances, the flexibility and focus of mind that we encounter when reading almost any *Rambler* essay. For Boswell, Johnson's style is the antithesis not only of Addison's, but also of Socrates' in the Platonic dialogues, because it does not 'reduce ... philosophy to the simplicity of common life' (156). But Boswell's difficulty, in these instances, in connecting Johnson's language with thought, and thought with experience, is part of his general portrait of Johnson's character under consideration in this chapter. Boswell's perception of Johnson's style fundamentally shapes the image of Johnson given in the biography, because Johnson the man and Johnson the writer are not separable, though they are different, and connected to each other at the deepest levels of character and soul.

Hawkins had remarked how Johnson's 'conversation style bore a great resemblance to that of his writings', and how many who had made collections of his sayings in order to capture Johnson's particular energy, 'rendered ... the collections ... of little worth' because they lacked the requisite capacity (163). Boswell set out to rectify that situation in the belief that he had that capacity. Yet Boswell's criticism of Johnson's works bears the same marks of the interiority of his recreation of Johnson's conversations — a quality which places him as much beyond any other biographer in dramatising Johnson's conversation as it places him below many critics in reading Johnson's works. For Boswell is unable to feel and to articulate the connection between Johnson's writing and his character, and therefore some essential part of Johnson's thought, of his soul — represented by the experiential substantiality that is embodied in his language and that makes him a radically different kind of man and thinker from the one portrayed by Boswell — is silently excluded from Boswell's portrait of Johnson's mind and character. This process of selecting and interpreting is no more and no less than that which governs every biographical and critical assessment of Johnson. It underlies perhaps the single greatest weakness of the *Life of Johnson*. Yet it also informs the self-consistency and coherence of Boswell's idea of Johnson that, in the opinion of many, is the basis of Boswell's greatness as a biographer.

But Johnson is a great *writer*. Notwithstanding the complex relations between life and work, Johnson's writing embodies a fundamental part of his mind and soul unavailable elsewhere. Boswell opened the *Life* by referring to Johnson as 'him who excelled all mankind in writing the lives of others' (19), yet the *Life of Johnson* does not attempt to follow Johnson's lead in the *Lives of the Poets* (1779–81), which Boswell called 'the richest, most beautiful, and indeed most perfect production of Johnson's pen' (801): 'This is the work of all Dr Johnson's writings will perhaps be read most generally, and with most pleasure' (1090). The difference between Johnson's *Lives* and Boswell's *Life* points to Boswell's originality, and, at the same time, to what limits him as a reader of Johnson's works, and as a writer of his life. The difference between the *Lives* and the *Life* also represents a change in cultural sensibility at the end of the eighteenth century.

Strictly speaking Johnson has no *a priori*, single idea of the poets whose lives he depicts, and he has no need to identify with them emotionally. While he accepts the given poet's mortality as part of nature − a debt owed − and treats the significant events of the man's life on their own terms in one section of a Life, while he discusses the man's poetry on its terms in another section of the Life; the character of the man − what might be described as the man's truth and essence − is not striven for, but allowed to come into focus in the encounter between life and work which the structure of the *Lives* effect (see Greg Clingham, 'Johnson's Dryden', in *Dryden and Others*, ed. Earl Miner (Cambridge, 1992)).

The 'truth' that Johnson finds in each poet's life − in Milton, Dryden, Pope, Swift, Gray − is located in nature, not created by the mind, a realm separated from the natural and the historical, as it is in Boswell's portrait of Johnson's character. So the character of Pope or Dryden or Milton in the *Lives* is not felt to be personal in any narrow sense (despite, for example, Johnson's antagonism towards Milton the man) − even while these characters have come into being as a result of personal statements of judgement and experience by Johnson at every stage of his work. For through his capacity to see life and art as continuous though different, within the framework of general nature, Johnson discovers the human revelatory powers of literature represented by the works of the poets who form his subject. This embodied perception of the continuity between life and work in the *Lives* separates Johnson from Boswell fundamentally. It represents a difference in personal and intellectual temperament, as well as a radical cultural shift, that Boswell's biography attempts to understand and bridge as part of the process of recollecting Johnson in biography. The integral presence of an 'independent' aspect of a man's life in the *Lives*, in which the poet speaks for his own deepest intuitions and understanding of life through his art, gives a sense of permanence and substantiality to Johnson's portraits. The story Johnson tells of the lives of his poets is not likely to veer off into fiction — as Boswell's scenes sometimes do — partly because the poet has contributed, in a most profound and impersonal way, to the telling of his own story. We do not have the 'historical' Dryden (or Milton or Pope) before us, but Johnson's fictional portrayal of their lives feels true for these individual poets, because true for humanity in general.

Boswell does not notice the dynamic relationship between life and work in the *Lives*, that Johnson holds together within his general nature and the structure of the work. For the division between thought and style which Boswell sees in *Rasselas* and the *Rambler*, he echoes when writing about the *Lives*: Johnson, he says, 'had little more to do than to put his thoughts upon paper, exhibiting first each Poet's life, and then subjoining a critical examination of his genius and works' (1090). At the same time, in his biography Boswell does not permit Johnson the freedom to tell his own story. Boswell does use Johnson's letters as evidence of his experience, to an unprecedented extent. But he does not believe that what, in the nineteenth century, Hallam Tennyson found true for his real father could be true for his, Boswell's, spiritual father: 'besides the letters of my father and of his friends there are his poems, and in these we must look for the innermost sanctuary of his being. For my own part, I feel strongly that no biographer could so truly give him as he gives himself in his own works' (*Alfred Lord Tennyson: A Memoir*, 2 vols. (1897), I, xi). Strangely, the vital continuity between Johnson's life and writing is something that Boswell claimed for *himself* in the memoir he published in the *European Magazine* (May 1791): 'In giving an account of this Gentleman [i.e. himself], there is little occasion to make private inquiries; as from a certain peculiarity, frank, open, and ostentatious, which he avows, his history, like that of the old Seigneur Michael de

Montaigne, is to be traced in his writings' (Pottle, *Literary Career* xxix).

The conclusion to this brief consideration of Boswell as a critic of Johnson's works is clear. Johnson's works are not really integral to Boswell's portrait of Johnson; or rather, Boswell's commentary on Johnson's works is part of a larger imaginative and personal process by which Boswell defines an idea of Johnson the Christian hero, the great and good man. Boswell describes this idea metaphorically as a process of mummification (see above, pp. 28–9). At the same time, Johnson's writing is resistant to that kind of assimilation. So Boswell's final portrait of Johnson's character, *tour de force* though it is, cannot really carry the weight or capture the integral nature of Johnson's character as articulated through his own writing. Instead, as we have seen, Boswell proposes a division between world and spirit sublimated by transcendence – 'In proportion to the native vigour of the mind, the contradictory qualities will be the more prominent, and more difficult to be adjusted ...' Boswell's praise for Johnson's 'art of thinking, the art of using his mind', that gives rise to a 'knowledge [which] ... was, in him, true, evident, and actual wisdom' (1400–1), is generous and eloquent. But these sentiments require Johnson's writing – the substance of his experience in his thought and syntax – to give full meaning to the 'wisdom' and the 'intimate acquaintance with human nature' that Boswell defines as Johnson's distinguishing features. For it is only in Johnson's writing, at the point where mind meets world, and the individual self and general nature become one, that the 'contradictory qualities' will be seen to be more than authentic eccentricities that can be subsumed by mind or spirit.

Hume's importance in the *Life*

The transcendence of the mind and spirit, and the particular presence that Boswell's art associates with that mode of being, is important in the *Life* for two related reasons already mentioned: it defines a focus for Boswell's self-definition in relation to Johnson's end (end in the sense of the purpose of Johnson's life as well as his death); and it focuses Boswell's doubts about scepticism, epitomised by the life and philosophy of David Hume (1711–76). Hume is also Johnson's main antagonist in the world of the *Life*. Boswell's use of Johnson as an antagonist to Hume shrewdly perceives how much of Johnson's thought is formulated as an implicit answer to Hume, and in the *Life* Boswell is interested in Johnson's exemplary battle with the sceptical, Humean side of himself. For Hume, a Scotsman, a lapsed Calvinist, a Tory humanist, and also the most radical and famous philosopher in Britain in the eighteenth century, was greatly admired by Boswell, and represented one powerful side of his own personal and cultural psyche. Hume's philosophy and cultural persona were, in a sense, the Enlightened Scottish way of dealing with the threat to its political and cultural identity represented by the hegemony of England. It was a means of subverting and appropriating the authority of the paternal, politically powerful cultural institutions of England by enlisting the support of a radically different European cultural praxis.

Though it is impossible to do justice to Hume's thought here, it is necessary, for understanding Boswell, to note the powerful effect of his scepticism on Boswell's thinking. In the *Treatise of Human Nature* Hume argued that we can know nothing for certain beyond our own experience, and that we have no rational basis for knowledge of ultimate, absolute truths (such as Christianity and British political traditions had taken for granted), nor for our moment-to-moment connection with the ordinary world in which we live. What gives coherence and meaning to our experience is the force of habit, constructed by the memory and the imagination, which, however, tell us about what happens within the human mind, not what happens in the world outside, nor about our real connection to that world.

In terms of personal identity (and, by extension, historical and cultural unity and continuity) Hume's scepticism leaves the individual precariously balanced 'betwixt a false reason and none at all' (*Treatise* I.vii, 268). While his scepticism maintains that the knowledge of things 'in themselves' and of causes and effects amount to nothing but knowledge of our own mind, it 'cuts off all hope', and leads to potential nihilism:

The *intense* view of these manifold contradictions and imperfections in human reason has so wrought upon me, and heated my brain, that I am ready to reject all belief and reasoning, and can look upon no opinion even as more probable or likely than another. Where am I, or what? From what causes do I derive my existence, and to what condition shall I return? ... I am confounded with all these questions, and begin to fancy myself in the most deplorable condition imaginable, inviron'd with the deepest darkness, and utterly depriv'd of the use of every member and faculty.   (268–9)

At this point, where reason is unable to disentangle contradictions or light up darkness, 'nature' steps in: 'Most fortunately it happens, that since reason is incapable of dispelling these clouds, nature herself suffices to that purpose, and cures me of this philosophical melancholy and delirium, either by relaxing this bent of mind, or by some avocation, and lively impression of my senses, which obliterate all these chimeras' (269). This undercutting his own arguments, by invoking nature to balance the inadequacies of reason, is a stroke of great and delicate wit on Hume's part; it is, as he says, the cleverest manifestation of his sceptical principles: 'I may, nay I must yield to the current of nature, in submitting to my senses and understanding [even though they are fallacious]; and in this blind submission I shew most perfectly my sceptical disposition and principles' (269).

Hume's nature is delicate and ambiguous. If it operates purposefully in filling up the emptiness uncovered by philosophical scepticism, it also offers nothing more solid or more principled by which to live than common opinion: 'to live, and talk, and act like other people in the common affairs of life' (269). The implicit opposition, then, between thinking (reason) and living (nature) in Hume's thought is resolved in his wit; or, rather, the peculiar poise and disengaged insouciance he cultivates holds these entities together in a state of perpetually possible (but not actual) dissolution and meaninglessness.

Hume cannot believe in a whole, integrated self, nor in a decentred, disintegrated self; the urbane, civilised poise of his prose is his way of being in between these states, inhabiting neither.

This intelligent, sceptical poise is one way Hume deals with the threat of Calvinist absolutes. Since (as Manning argues) causality is a mere interpretation of events, Hume sees reason as either passive and precluding the possibility of an active relation to the world, or as actually creating its own world (*Puritan–Provincial Vision* 39). Hume here behaves like the Calvinist who 'desires to make an inscrutable universe "mean"' by emphasising the mind's autonomy in nothingness: 'in the absence of divine sanctions and the guilt associated with the split between appearance and reality, Hume can allow his mind to play freely over the implications of its own non-existence' (Manning 39, 41). This, however, is a way of eliding endings. I suggest that the fear of endings and of the loneliness of individuality – and, within the context of Calvinist theology, the fear of retribution and judgement associated with those limits – is psychologised and sublimated in Hume's thought. Scepticism and nature are invoked to palliate the experience of spiritual abandonment and loneliness:

I am first affrighted and confounded with that forelorn solitude, in which I am plac'd in my philosophy, and fancy myself some strange uncouth monster, who not being able to mingle and unite in society, has been expell'd all human commerce, and left utterly abandon'd and disconsolate ... When I turn my eye inward, I find nothing but doubt and ignorance. (264)

These words describe Calvinist experience in the eighteenth century, including Boswell's (see Manning 38–46). But Boswell was unable to cultivate the detachment, the 'enlightened' critical intelligence of Hume's style of dealing with these spiritual challenges. He was less able to deconstruct them than modern criticism thinks. Of course, Hume's sceptical detachment was not confined to his writing, for he had a reputation amongst contemporaries for indifference towards mortality, as Boswell's interview with Hume on his death-bed confirms (3 March 1777; *Extremes* 11–15).

This interview, and the near-hysteria it generates in Boswell, prompts the discussion about death between Boswell and Johnson on 17 September 1777 (*Life* 838–9), just as Hume's attitude to death occasioned the conversation between Boswell and Johnson on 26 October 1769 (see above, pp. 53–5). On the earlier occasion Boswell brings up the point that Hume denied fearing death on the basis that he was no more troubled by not existing after death than he was by not existing before his birth (a Lucretian view, effectively summarising the argument of Hume's essay 'On the Immortality of the Soul', (*Life* 426–7)). In the 'interview' with Hume, Boswell is 'shocked' that in the very face of death he was 'placid and even cheerful' (*Extremes* 11) and maintained his poise – his 'infidelity', as Boswell says (*Life* 838). Hume responds to Boswell's 'curiosity to be satisfied if he persisted in disbelieving a future state even when he had death before his eyes', by applying his published sceptical principles to that particular question, and by engaging Boswell in witty banter (*Extremes* 11–13).

In response to both of Boswell's accounts, Johnson does not try to refute Hume philosophically, by attempting, for example, to prove that reason can certainly unravel the nature of God and the hereafter. Johnson's own fears of death and knowledge of the human mind permit him no easy intellectual refutation. What he does is to incorporate his experience of the weakness of the mind and the need for assurance – phenomena taken by Hume as evidence for the *absence* of any truth beyond the self – into an image of human nature connected to history and to the material practicalities of living, and thereby accepts and affirms a 'redemption' of human weakness. He says of Hume's indifference, 'It is more probable that he should assume an appearance of ease, than that so very improbable a thing should be, as a man not afraid of going (as, in spite of his delusive theory, he cannot be sure he may go) into an unknown state, and not being uneasy at leaving all he knew' (838–9). For Johnson, to leave 'all one knows', one's manifold connection to the particulars of material and intellectual life, underlies a vision of nature (reminiscent of Augustine and Pascal) as fallen, but *therefore* susceptible of grace and redemption. For Hume, all religious principles are chimerical because nature is impenetrable by reason, it is devoid of any philosophical coherence which might form the basis for action. Hume's 'nature' — his decision to 'live, and talk, and act like other people in the common affairs of life' — turns out to be a source of moral guidance negatively arrived at. Johnson labelled it as 'vanity' (including perhaps the dual sense of vanity as helplessness and as pride), and connected it with a French Enlightenment style of thinking and writing (310, 314, 838). Hume's sceptical poise, even while invoking 'nature', acknowledges how little of himself he is prepared to trust to anything other than himself.

Boswell could not understand Hume, yet his shock — his mingled horror and fascination — at Hume's attitude on his death-bed expresses emotionally the human shortcomings of Hume's philosophical logic. Because it provides no moral, human support in the face of an individual's existential helplessness, Hume's solitude is, for Boswell, almost as troublesome as the fear of endings and judgement that it is designed to obviate. Boswell is caught between Johnson and Hume, casting the two as equally powerful representatives of different attitudes towards life and death. All the ideals with which the *Life* invests Johnson, or which it discovers in him, exist within the wider context constituted by Hume, the greatest Scotsman of the eighteenth century whose Life Boswell thought of writing. Johnson's presence in the *Life* is the antithesis of Hume's detachment. If Hume's scepticism is a way of eliding endings, it is also a way of dealing with the demands of the material world and the body. Hume's scepticism sublimates them in the very process of — as he says — 'yield[ing] to the current of nature' (*Treatise* 269). But Boswell neither wishes to nor can he perform the same tricks with Johnson's presence and with the implications for himself of his own bodily connection to experience. For Boswell, Johnson's presence as constructed in the *Life* is a guarantee of his personal identity and security. In its antithesis to Hume it reveals how the *Life* elaborates a mythical cultural history for Scotland

that displaces Hume (as cultural guru), displaces the fathers of
Scottish culture (including Lord Auchinleck, Boswell's father),
by *his* elaborate image of Johnson. It is in Boswell's treatment
of Johnson's end, therefore, that many of the issues discussed
in this book come together.

The *Life*'s double ending: biography as ritual

The last five months of Johnson's life (July–December 1784),
from Boswell's last leave-taking to Johnson's death, comprise
about eighty pages in the World's Classics edition (about 100
pages in the Hill-Powell edition). In these pages Boswell *twice*
goes over the approach to Johnson's death, on both occasions
(the first comprising pages 1324–77, the second pages 1377–
402) marking significant last events (such as Johnson's last visit
to Lichfield) and specific periods before Johnson's death (e.g.,
'About eight or ten days before his death ...,' 'three or four days
only before his death ...'). This double attempt at recording,
accepting, and understanding Johnson's death is emotionally
interesting. Naturally, the entire section is elegiac – a tone
covering feelings which Boswell described as 'most difficult and
dangerous' and which made him 'very anxious' (1378).

The first part of this section opens with an especially poignant
depiction of the last parting of Johnson and Boswell, an
epitome of Boswell's entire emotional relation to Johnson.
Boswell's view is consciously retrospective, feelingly aware
of the distance between now and then, and therefore adding
great significance to that past moment:

He asked me whether I would go with him to his house; I declined
it, from apprehension that my spirits would sink. We bade adieu
to each other affectionately in the carriage. When he had got down
upon the foot-pavement, he called out, 'Fare you well'; and without
looking back, sprung away with a kind of pathetick briskness,
if I may use that expression, which seemed to indicate a struggle
to conceal uneasiness, and impressed me with a foreboding of our
long, long separation.   (1326)

This passage is one of many in the *Life* which raise fundamental questions about the objectivity and the truth of what

Boswell depicts about Johnson; for the struggle and uneasiness recorded above are as much Boswell's as they are Johnson's. The pain and foreboding of 30 June 1784 (the day on which they parted for the last time) are being recalled and assimilated emotionally and psychologically by the act of looking backwards from 1791, when the passage was written. The passage proposes and assimilates several perspectives. Boswell offers us the perspective of the detached narrator, reporting a past event, controlling the emotional energy of the parting through reported speech ('He asked me ...'), recognising the feelings arising in himself, but keeping them outside the self by keeping them in the past ('apprehension that my spirits *would* sink'). At the same time the passage recognises a fact, typically enforced by a single, telling piece of direct speech: 'Fare you well.' This has the effect of acknowledging the eternal presence of the parting, of recording the distance between Johnson and Boswell, and then of closing the distance between the two as the prose focuses the consciousness within Boswell. Boswell acknowledges the power of the feelings 'then', by letting them in now: Johnson's 'pathetick briskness' and 'struggle to conceal uneasiness' reveal not only what Johnson's feelings might have been but how Boswell remembers and sees Johnson now. Boswell's 'apprehension' is finally acknowledged, and the effect is to bring him into the present, in a fashion that eclipses the apparent limitations of memory.

The 'long, long separation', Johnson's end and absence, is the main great event in the *Life*, and creates the conditions that make biography possible. 'Separation' makes it possible for Boswell to 'recollect' and to immortalise Johnson, as both the opening and the closing sections of the *Life* indicate is Boswell's mythic purpose.

Still, the *fact* of Johnson's death is ambiguously related to Boswell's capacity for recall. For within the imaginative, theological world of the *Life*, Johnson's presence represents forgiveness for Boswell, while Johnson's absence removes the possibility of grace. Therefore, in several ways the closing section of the *Life* enacts the paradoxical relation between retribution and redemption central to the eighteenth-century

Calvinist consciousness (Manning, *Puritan–Provincial Vision* 6–15). It does so by asking whether Johnson, the Christian hero, will die in such a way as to manifest the apotheosis wished for by Boswell. It does so too by invoking Boswell's larger experience, which locates the *Life* in the context of his whole psychological, familial, and cultural history. Moreover, the double ending of the *Life* represents a recognition (now orthodox due to the work of such historiographers as Hayden White, Lionel Gossman, and Dominick LaCapra) that history is fictionally constructed – that 'past' experience may support different stories and be emplotted and understood in different ways. This is Boswell's deliberate attempt to place himself in relation to his past, and thereby to create an independent set of responses to life, different from those dictated by his family and the legal and political establishments of Scotland and England.

The correspondence between Boswell and Johnson in the last few weeks of Johnson's life demonstrates the paradoxes mentioned above (1360–3). From this correspondence Boswell selects only portions to print as he thinks 'proper' (1360). Once (26 July 1784) he acknowledges having written to Johnson in 'dejection and fretfulness' about Johnson's illness, as if it were a personal reproach to himself, and expressing fears for Johnson based on a dream he had (1361). Johnson's reply – only partly printed (since the *Life* is the source for this and other letters, the suppressed portion of Johnson's reply has not come to light) – is direct and challenges Boswell's melancholy ('write like a man'), but he is also encouraging and warm: 'Write to me often ... I consider your fidelity and tenderness as a great part of the comforts which are yet left to me ... life is very short and very uncertain; let us spend it as well as we can' (1361). But this is not comforting enough for Boswell, so he (intentionally or unintentionally – see note, *Life* 1361) imagines Johnson sending him another letter on 28 July to apologise for his harshness, to which Boswell replies 'conjur[ing] him not to do me the injustice of charging me with affectation' (1362). But then Boswell goes silent for a long time – perhaps he sulks, for he says 'it was not, or at least I thought it was not, in my power to write to my illustrious friend' (1362). Boswell 'much regret[ted]' this silence, perhaps because it later seemed like a missed opportunity. But after receiving Johnson's last letter, dated 3 November 1784, which still dealt harshly with his melancholy (in a passage also not printed by Boswell), Boswell writes two 'kind letters as I could', the last of which, however, Johnson did not receive before his death (1362–3).

After Johnson's death Boswell is 'consoled' for all of this stressful lack of communication by 'being informed that [Johnson] spoke of me on his death-bed, with affection, and I look forward with humble hope of renewing our friendship in a better world' (1363). Though Boswell excellently dramatises scenes at which he is not present himself, when Johnson is on his death-bed, at this point in the *Life*, right at the end of the first section dealing with Johnson's end, the focus is clearly on Boswell, and then on an afterlife, not on the dying Johnson. Boswell's personal, emotional vision of the end loses sight of a separate, mundane Johnson. Here, too, is where Boswell takes formal leave of the reader, for having brought to a close the mortal life of Johnson, he says the 'peculiar plan of [the] biographical undertaking' means that his presence is no longer necessary (1363).

But Boswell does not subsequently absent himself from the narrative, but changes his relation to events when recounting the second part of the closing section of the *Life*. This part begins with a long footnote by Boswell detailing the works that Johnson did *not* write (1363–6), in which the biographical text vanishes for four pages; then there are passages on Johnson's Classical learning (1367), his imitators (1368–73), and on his feelings for his departed friends (1373). The focus switches from the person of Johnson to his accomplishments, and to the perpetuation of his memory via his imitators. Donna Heiland has discussed how the fragmentation of Boswell's text at this point 'images [the] fragmentation and scattering of Johnson's body' even while it 'makes sure that his text, and its subject, will always be reconstituted by the reader as well' ('Remembering the Hero' 200). This manner of commemorating Johnson leads Boswell to consider Johnson's commemoration in his last few weeks of those who had been particularly close to him, his parents and his brother, and his wife, Tetty.

However, at this point Johnson's imminent death is so significant for Boswell that he cannot read Johnson's actions *or* words with clarity. He imagines Johnson's consciousness as guilt-ridden, and his actions as placatory: 'Johnson's affection for his departed relations seemed to grow warmer as he approached nearer to the time when he might hope to see them again. It probably appeared to him that he should upbraid himself with unkind inattention, were he to leave the world without having paid a tribute of respect to their memory' (1373). He quotes two of Johnson's letters; the first concerns a stone in the Lichfield parish church to commemorate his family (2 December 1784):

I have enclosed the Epitaph for my Father, Mother, and Brother, to be all engraved on the large size, and laid in the middle aisle in St Michael's church, which I request the clergyman and church-wardens to permit.

The first care must be to find the exact place of interment, that the stone may protect the bodies. Then let the stone be deep, massy, and hard; and do not let the difference of ten pounds, or more, defeat our purpose. (1373–4)

The second letter is to Lucy Porter, Tetty's daughter by her first marriage, about the stone, with epitaph, that Johnson had laid over her grave in Kent. Boswell quotes the letter, but omits Johnson's English translation of the Latin epitaph (Johnson himself excludes the Latin from the letter). From *The Letters of Samuel Johnson* (ed. R. W. Chapman, 3 vols. (Oxford, 1958)) we discover the epitaph to have been as follows:

Here lie the remains of Elizabeth, descended from the ancient house of Jarvis at Peatling in Leicestershire; a Woman of beauty, elegance, ingenuity, and piety. Her first Husband was Henry Porter; her second, Samuel Johnson, who having loved her much, and lamented her long, laid this stone upon her.

She died in March. 1752.

(III, 252)

Johnson's words in both letters contrast with Boswell's picture of him at this point. Boswell sees Johnson's actions in the context of a Christian afterlife, suffused with Calvinist consciousness. Johnson did not want to 'upbraid himself with unkind inattention'. Boswell sees Johnson's actions as motivated by a search of expiation. But Johnson's letters are remarkable, and exceptionally beautiful and moving, for their pure factuality, their simple attention to the things of this world – to the size, weight, and texture of the stone that will protect the bodies of his family; to the *difference* that his wife made for him in this life. Tetty lived and died, and the stone Johnson lays upon her commemorates his love and his lamentation, both as durable as that stone. The epitaph begins with her 'remains' and ends with her date of death, and though there is absolutely nothing other-worldly about Johnson's words, they enact a deep religious experience of the oneness of spirit and body in *this* life, of the mysterious difference and continuity of history and Providence implicit in his nature.

Johnson's nature is no more Boswell's than it is Hume's. From this point in the *Life* Boswell twice more, dramatically, tries to recount Johnson's death ('Samuel Johnson preparing himself for that doom ...', 1374 and 1378). The narrative becomes strung out, fragmented (1378–88), as if this might be a way of holding on to Johnson, keeping in touch with Johnson physically by having his fragmented text metonymically enact a consumption of the body of Johnson's text, Johnson's body (see Heiland). Just before the description of Johnson's funeral, Boswell's process of consumption takes an unusual turn:

A few days before his death, he had asked Sir John Hawkins, as one of his executors, where he should be buried; and on being answered 'Doubtless, in Westminster-Abbey,' seemed to feel a satisfaction, very natural to every man of any imagination, who has no family sepulchre in which he can be laid with his fathers.

(1393–4)

This juxtaposition between men of imagination and men of family with private sepulchres focuses the identification with and an exaggerated independence from Johnson that coexist in the *Life* and that, I have argued, are integral to Boswell's relation to Johnson. Yet now that Johnson is dead, and 'He has made a chasm, which not only nothing can fill up, but which nothing has a tendency to fill up' (1394–5), Boswell's sepulchre seems vacuous and no compensation for what he has lost. The end of the *Life* records what is very difficult for Boswell, and is, in its complex honesty, an impressive piece of historical and fictional writing.

Boswell's complex position at the end of the *Life* might, then, be summarised as follows. The symbolic and personal importance that Johnson represents for Boswell raises the question of love. One of the powers of love is its capacity both to recall and to undo the past – psychologically and emotionally to find in the beloved both stimulation to recall one's earliest experiences, and a desire to have him or her compensate for all the earliest emotional and psychic deprivations. I have demonstrated how Boswell's need of and reverence for Johnson point to his difficulty in completely accepting his death. Johnson simply mattered too much for the biographer who was always, even at the end of his life, a young man. On one level, the end of the *Life* takes us right back to the beginning of Boswell's recorded relationship with Johnson, for the concluding portrait of his character is closely modelled on the portrait beginning the *Tour to the Hebrides* (an echo to which Boswell explicitly draws attention). On another level, Boswell's narrative, and his imaginative recreation of Johnson, appropriate and consume Johnson in a pseudo-religious ritual in which the celebrant and worshipper consumes the god, and thereby assures political and historical embodiment for the god and a kind of immortality for himself (Heiland, in *New Light* 199–203). On yet another level, Boswell's biography recalls and 're-members' Johnson in a feeling and artistic exploration of the *absence* of the man as means of imaginatively resurrecting the image of the hero who is the object of Boswell's thought, and thereby making Johnson the man present. This process of creative recollection encompasses a richly complex series of images, the way all good history and biography does, and it is deeply connected with personal, cultural, and religious motives in Boswell's unfolding experience, from the 1760s to the 1790s.

But the striving associated with psychological and emotional need to control and the need for existential security points to a disbelief in the substantiality of the recollection. Difficulty in accepting Johnson's death fully is in fact related to the difficulty in recalling Johnson. Acceptance presupposes a self, grounded in the world − a love of self that accepts its limits, its feelings, its own potential death, and, consequently, a self that generates and sustains all the meaningful relations with other people, with nature, with society, with God. Paradoxically, a deeper acceptance of Johnson's death would also be the clearest expression of Boswell's love for Johnson the man, and thus the condition on which he, Johnson, could be recalled, and Boswell the biographer be empowered and set free. Permitting Johnson the *writer* to have more of a say would have facilitated the process. By carefully controlling and selecting the aspects of Johnson's writings for comment Boswell permits only that part of Johnson to be heard that accords with his idea of who the man is and with his idea of the importance to be accorded to Johnson's work. The most elementary psychological understanding testifies to the double bind into which Boswell gets himself by such manipulation, notwithstanding his art.

The double bind, however, has its roots in serious and painful spiritual experience for Boswell. For his difficulty in recalling, 're-membering' Johnson, making him whole (rather than dismembering him), is proportionate to his difficulty in letting Johnson go. Johnson simply mattered too much to Boswell, and psychically his absence signified the absence of all meaning to Boswell. The great spiritual and ontological significance that Boswell attaches to Johnson's presence, discussed in different ways in this book, is another way of noting Boswell's fixation on Johnson's body psychically accompanying the related struggle for selfhood and independence. The text of the *Life* metonymically consumes this body in order to produce, through art, its ideal, pseudo-transcendental image of Johnson. In what he includes Boswell is as selective as any real poet is, yet he feels compelled to *affirm* that he records everything, because the least loss of detail *seems* unbearable to one who venerates Johnson as he does: 'I cannot allow any fragment whatever that floats in my memory concerning the great subject of this work to be lost' (868). And of his last conversation and dinner with Johnson, Boswell regretfully says: 'Had I known that this was the last time I should enjoy in this world, the conversation of a friend whom I so much respected, and from whom I derived so much instruction and entertainment, I should have been deeply affected. When I now look back to it, I am vexed that a single word should have been forgotten' (1325). As so often in this complex book, the vexation – the artistically presented image – compensates for the 'deep affect[ion]' of the historical moment. Nevertheless, Boswell's yearning and the images he uses betray a certain absence of Johnson's spirit: the *Life* 'will be an Egyptian Pyramid in which there will be a compleat mummy of Johnson that Literary Monarch' (see above, p. 29). An embalmed body, under Boswell's control, but body without spirit. Therefore, moving as the depiction of Johnson's last days are (see also 1324), interesting as Boswell's artistic image of Johnson is, and compelling as his own history is in the work, the *Life of Johnson* is unable to 're-member' some essential aspect of Johnson's character.

When all is said and done, however, the relationship between Boswell and Johnson did amount to a mutually supportive friendship lasting twenty-one years, during which time Boswell may have sought the satisfaction of his needs in Johnson's presence, but he also demonstrated to the well-being of his friend a commitment, spiritedness, and tenacity which are very rare in a modern world of excitement, instant satisfaction, and the exercise of power. One moving aspect of Boswell's *Life* is the great evidence it gives for the need to humanise power if people are to be civilised with each other and to live at peace with themselves. That he wasn't able to achieve his ideals fully makes the work more interesting because it leaves an opening for the reader to enter and learn about his or her own experience. Those who take easy satisfaction in knocking Boswell down should perhaps remember that for all Johnson's superiority he too needed what his young friend could give: 'You must be as much with me as you can. You have done me good. You cannot think how much better I am since you came in' (1195).

Chapter 6

Boswell's modernity

Boswell's sensibility is very congenial to modern readers. The duality of his biographical artifice is part of a cultural change at the end of the eighteenth and the beginning of the nineteenth centuries of which the twentieth century is the inheritor. Locating Boswell's position in that change is to trace one line of influence of the *Life* in its 'afterlife'.

First, Boswell's biographical method anticipates the idea of the continuity of historical and fictional narrative advocated by modern theorists of narrative, such as Hayden White, Louis Mink, and Paul Ricoeur. White and Mink urge that historical narrative exercises a mediative function; it shapes a symbolic and metaphoric structure, where narrative constitutes and not merely records the historical object realistically (White, *Tropics of Discourse* (Baltimore, 1978), 91, 95; Mink, *Historical Understanding*, ed. Fay, Golob, and Vann (Ithaca, 1987), 197, 201). These theories are manifestly borne out in Boswell's narrative. Though Boswell knows that fact and fiction are not incompatible − knows, that is, that the authenticity of Johnson's life that he seeks to embody and convey depends upon artistic mediation − he nonetheless feels a tension between these entities (Clingham, 'Truth and Artifice'). This tension reflects a split in historiographical thinking evident after the French Revolution (White 123).

The tension between fact and fiction, truth and artifice, and between mind and nature implicit in Boswell's treatment of human experience in the *Life* is partly resolved in the composite image of Johnson's character offered by the *Life*. Boswell's image of Johnson guarantees his selfhood and functionality on several levels. In political terms, Johnson's moral authority and traditional Tory and Anglican principles represent for Boswell a bulwark against the 'horrible anarchy' he associated with the French Revolution (the anarchic violence of which was clear by 1793, when the second edition of the *Life* appeared), and the rebelliousness it might engender amongst radicals and reformers in Britain (Brady 421, 427). '[Johnson's] strong, clear, and animated enforcement of religion, morality, loyalty, and subordination ... will ... prove an effectual antidote to that detestable sophistry which has been lately imported from France, under the false name of PHILOSOPHY, and with a malignant industry has been employed against the peace, good order, and happiness of society, in our free and prosperous country' (7). Typically, the political differences between Boswell and Johnson (on, for example, the American Revolution and slavery, both of which Boswell supported and Johnson opposed) did not prevent Boswell from enlisting Johnson's moral authority ideologically.

That authority is present in Boswell's narrative in subtle political ways. Though the question of Johnson's and Boswell's political allegiance to Jacobitism is a vexed question under investigation by Howard Erskine-Hill and others, it is clear, according to the artistic appropriation discussed in this book, that Boswell enlisted Johnson's authority as part of the process of elaborating for himself an independent, Scottish political identity. As an extension of that activity he elaborates a mythical history of Scotland in accordance with a romantic Jacobitism. Anti-revolutionary sentiment and Jacobitism blend in the *Life*. In the 1790s Boswell was writing a tragedy entitled *Favras* (never finished or published) about the trial and execution of the Marquis de Favras for conspiring against the revolutionary state in France. The undertaking, as Thomas Crawford notes, 'involved the sublimation of political emotions that had dominated him for many years. He had long run together retrospective feelings of Jacobite loyalty with the adoration of "Great George our King": now the heroism of a royalist martyr in France was to be linked to both sorts of *British* loyalty in a paean of praise to the constitution that had developed from the Glorious Revolution of 1688' (35, also 33–5). Subtly the principles associated with 1688 were advocated in the *Life*. But since the issue of monarchical (and, therefore, governmental) legitimacy in British politics declines in importance after the defeat of the 1745 Jacobite uprising, and the doctrine of contractarianism becomes blended with an older, more patriarchal, artistrocratic politics, the issue of the inherent and actual authority of the *de facto* government becomes central (see Clark 44–57).

While Boswell cultivates an English Toryism and Anglicanism (in opposition to his father and the Scottish Presbyterian establishment of which his father is part), and expresses the utmost admiration for George III and allegiance to the Hanoverians (of which his father approved), he also elaborates an imaginative world for himself that assimilates Johnson as father-figure and standard of authority, and that reconciles Boswell to his status as outsider vis-à-vis Scottish culture. The sentimental Jacobitism that Boswell expresses in his account, in the *Tour*, of the escape of Charles Edward Stuart from the Highlands after the battle of Culloden, and the credence he gives to James Macpherson's creation of Ossian in that attempt to give Scotland a glamorous and heroic past, are elements of a cultural nostalgia which, in the *Life*, appear as a spiritual homelessness. The function that Johnson plays in alleviating that homelessness administers to Boswell's political mythology, involving a union of father and son, of England and Scotland, under a moral, political, and social dispensation bodying forth political autonomy for native country and biographer.

But Hume-like, Boswell could never quite believe all this. The Christian-humanist tradition of Erasmus, More, Montaigne, Johnson, Cowley, and Dryden, and of which Johnson was, perhaps, the culmination, was a tradition of which Boswell was not part. Though, as Boswell reports, Johnson 'gives you a forcible hug, and shakes laughter out of you whether you will or no' (524), one never quite feels this in the *Life*. The presence, in Johnson, of the divine irresponsibility of Erasmus's goddess Folly is never felt in the *Life*. A central aspect of this absence is the imaginative and substantial absence of Johnson's works in the *Life*. Another is Boswell's recognition that his language runs up against a barrier, its own aporia, in trying to remember and recreate the definitive image of Johnson. So his attitude to Johnson's presence and authority is one of yearning and of recognising in them an essential aspect of his *own* nature towards which he strives but which he cannot embody.

This yearning has interesting Romantic coordinates. Theoretically, Boswell's *Sehnsucht* and its implicit dualism belong to the body of thought represented by German Idealistic historiography between the 1770s and 1850s, and to the associated doctrines of transcendental aesthetics of German and English Romantic literature. The implied historiography of the *Life* shares certain central principles with the thought of J.G. Herder (*Yet Another Philosophy of History For the Enlightenment of Mankind* (1774), *Ideas for a Philosophy of the History of Mankind* (1784–91)), Wilhelm von Humboldt ('On the Historian's Task' (1821)), and Leopold von Ranke (various manuscript lectures, such as 'On the Character of Historical Science' (1830s), published by G.G. Iggers and K. von Moltke in *The Theory and Practice of History* (New York, 1973)).

The principles of these German thinkers might be summed up as follows: historical phenomena are the external manifestation of underlying ideas; these ideas are neither abstract nor universally valid, but express themselves in concrete historical particulars, of which every individual and institution partakes; the historian understands each historical individuality in its uniqueness, by penetrating past its appearance to its inner structure. The spiritual apperception of the historian, as Ranke puts it (Iggers and Moltke 39), permits him to construct a truth only partly visible, and is facilitated by his language, which fuses the enquiring mind and the object of enquiry (Humboldt, 'On the Historian's Task', Iggers and Moltke 6–7). This theory enables a freedom of spirit for the historian engaged in hermeneutical reflection (discussed in H.-G. Gadamer's *Truth and Method* (New York, 1960), and exemplified in Schiller's essay on Universal History (1789)). It does so by asserting the plurality and relativity of human experience and human nature, and then identifying the inner nature of historical particulars and experience as being essentially of the quality of the mind. The historically distant and Other, and, in Christian terms (particularly apposite for Humboldt, Ranke, and Boswell), the fallen aspects of human nature and human experience are recalled and redeemed by virtue of their participation in the structure of the human mind, by their being made to transcend the limits of their place in nature.

The transcendence of the duality envisaged in German historiography (particularly the notion that in great writing, through the imagination, subject and object fuse, and enact a primal identity of world and mind), is argued by Friedrich Schelling in his *System of Transcendental Idealism* (1800). Rather than setting the mind over against nature, and articulating the relation of human nature to its limits, great writing reconciles nature and humankind:

Every fine painting comes into being through the removal of what one might call the invisible partition that separates the real from the ideal world; it is in itself no more than the gateway to the world of the imagination ... To the artist, nature is nothing other than that which it is to the philosopher, being only the ideal world as it appears under permanent restrictions, or only the imperfect reflection of a world that exists, not outside him, but within.

(quoted by Parker 78)

For artist read historian or biographer. This idealism is not complete in Boswell. But Schelling's reconciliation of the two worlds of the spirit and the senses – characteristic of other Romantic theorists, including Coleridge's *Biographia Literaria* and other works – reflects upon Boswell's dualism, and the striving for the integrity and nature he discovers in Johnson. The reconciliation of the two worlds of the senses and the spirit, of the historical and the poetic, is central to the definition of Romantic literature in A. W. von Schlegel's *Lectures on Dramatic Art and Literature* (1808) and Friedrich Schiller's *On Naive and Sentimental Poetry* (1795). Both describe the modern 'sentimental' attitude to nature by contrasting it with the ancient Greeks', but while Schiller believes that 'It is because nature in us has disappeared from humanity [that] we rediscover her in her truth only outside it' (103), Schlegel finds a different value in the situation Schiller describes.

The Christian culture, for Schlegel, surpasses the Greek by virtue of the consciousness it generates: 'Such a religion necessarily brings into full consciousness the intimation sleeping in every sensitive heart, the intimation that we aspire to a happiness unattainable here, that no external object can ever entirely satisfy our souls, and that all enjoyment is a momentary, fleeting illusion ... The poetry of the ancients was that of enjoyment, and ours is that of desire' (quoted by Parker 67).

Theoretically, Schlegel describes the very scenario which Boswell imagines for the particular experiences and for the entire life of Johnson as Christian hero. 'In proportion to the native vigour of the mind, the contradictory qualities will be the more prominent, and more difficult to be adjusted' (*Life* 1399). So Boswell imagines the process of 'adjustment' for Johnson's 'contradictory qualities' as being one in which spirit transcends nature – typologically and actually, in the form of a Christian apotheosis through death – rather than one in which spirit finds itself at home in the world of nature. Being at home in the world of present experience in all its fullness is what Johnson discovers Shakespeare's drama and Dryden's translations to facilitate. His own writing engenders the same kind of experience. Echoing the views of Schlegel, Boswell's historical narrative, however, emplots the trajectory of Johnson's life as a potential tragedy turned Christian romance, by stressing his moral freedom and intellectual greatness, and then the exemplary nature of Johnson's death in response to the potential helplessness of one subjected to the forces of the phenomenal world. This vision was a means of both palliating *and* justifying the moral and theological determinism Boswell was given to throughout his life, evidenced in his worries about death and control of life, a habit that Johnson took seriously but whose indulgence by Boswell (as we have seen in this book) also exasperated him.

Thus Boswell repeatedly tries to work through the spiritual homelessness characterising the *Life of Johnson* and other works, an attitude which the Romantic theorists, such as Schlegel and Schiller, and such Englightenment figures as Voltaire and Diderot saw as a form of superior, intelligent alienation. Just as Schlegel and the historiographers mentioned above elicit an idea of the creative, constitutive power of the mind to promote a greater penetration into the nature of existence and into the truth of the past, so Boswell's biographical method appeals to a similar set of ideals, thereby implicitly *and* explicitly arguing for greater insight into Johnson's life, and greater authenticity in the outcome. As he says, 'I cannot conceive a more perfect mode of writing any man's life ... I will venture to say that [Johnson] will be seen in this work more completely than any man who has ever yet lived' (*Life* 22). The ideological determinants of this contention have made Boswell very convincing and popular today, as well as the object of severe criticism by Johnsonians given to alternative ways of seeing Johnson.

Boswell and Diderot

The homelessness that underlies Boswell's art in the *Life* is very like the nephew's experience in Diderot's *Rameau's Nephew* (written 1761–74, but not published till the nineteenth century). This similarity takes several forms: it exists in the ways both characters – Rameau's nephew and Boswell in the *Life* – use pantomime and mimickry to control and appropriate the object of their attention. Pantomime, distinguished from acting by virtue of the *contrast* between its eloquence of gesture and its dumbness of language, is the essential structure of Boswell's imaginative activity, from the many pranks recorded in the journals, to his behaviour as a barrister, to his manner of imitating and recreating Johnson in the *Life* once he had been 'impregnated with the Johnsonian aether'. The double consciousness of Boswell's journals, and the dualism of the *Life*, are implicit in his essays on acting (published in *The London Magazine* (1770)). The power by which a player 'really is the character he represents' takes on a 'kind of double feeling' in which the 'feelings and passions of the character which he represents must take full possession as it were of the antechamber of his mind, while his own character remains in the innermost recess' ('Profession of a Player' 18).

As in Calvinist consciousness, self watches self acting out a drama for which there are no adequate words, and therefore only the muteness of what Johnson called the pantomime's 'power of universal mimickry' (*Dictionary*). As I have argued in earlier chapters, the capacity for the self to be both actor and audience in the drama of life is indicative of the tone and feeling of the efforts at self-articulation in the *Life* and journals, as it is of Boswell's legal practice.

This silent, eloquent double consciousness also characterises the nephew in Diderot's book, only the relation between his debasement and aggrandisement, between the self-contempt at his incredible pantomimic performance and his consequent empowerment, is more deeply, ambiguously fused. One reason for the greater ironic freedom generated by Rameau's nephew is the dialectical nature of the Socratic-type dialogue through which Diderot (the author) makes the nephew and Diderot-*moi* (the character) engage over idealism and materialism, over morality and aesthetics. The nephew, however, lives more ironically and deeply precariously within the realm constituted by his art − an art which he employs radically as a means of arguing for the primacy of morality over aesthetics, the good over the beautiful.

The ambiguities of the mediacy of art trouble Boswell more than they do Rameau's nephew (or Diderot): art is necessary for the freedom he seeks, yet it also potentially imprisons the self within self-consciousness; art is necessary to attain the ideals of nature proposed by Schlegel and Schiller as the goals of the modern Romantic, yet it uncovers an emptiness in language and a loneliness, disembodiment, and homelessness in the self. Richard Steele defines the pantomime's essential loneliness: 'This Pantomime may be said to be a Species of himself: He has no Commerce with the rest of Mankind, but as they are the Objects of Imitation' (*Tatler* 51, 1723 ed., II, 4). In dramatising these dilemmas shared by many European writers in the late eighteenth century, Boswell mirrors the self-reflexive relativity characteristic of our modern attitude towards literary language and the humanities, yet he also records the distress of the possibility of life without God, and hence without something to limit and validate his experience of self and world. The ironic, enlightened balance that Diderot establishes between aesthetics and morality, between art and life, was theoretically resolved in German idealism and historiography in the nineteenth century. Boswell was unable to reproduce a unity in his attempt in the *Life* to reconcile his art with Johnson's life.

There is, however, a Socratic element in the *Life* echoing Diderot's use of the dialogue in *Rameau's Nephew*. For, unlike any other biographer, Boswell spotted a wisdom in Johnson which he recognised could not be expressed in writing, and which could only come into the world through the kind of mediation that Socrates practised in the Platonic dialogues – that is, in conversation. That Boswell was not *quite* able to capture the Johnsonian substance in his conversations is as much due to Johnson's Socratic wisdom as it is to Boswell's inability. Perhaps no biographer could.

Boswell and Eckermann

It is to Boswell's credit that the same adverse judgement is not made about Johann Eckermann's *Conversations with Goethe* (1836 and 1848), one of the major works of European literature with which the *Life* asks to be compared. Because Eckermann is less ambitious in portraying Goethe, the great man of European letters, than Boswell is in portraying the great man of English letters, he risks less.

In scope and form the *Conversations* belongs more strictly to the genre of table-talk than to the full-scale biographical form that the *Life of Johnson* standardised. Its aim is slighter, and chronologically it covers a small period (only nine years). Yet Eckermann's artistic presentation of Goethe's speech distinguishes his work from table-talk such as Coleridge's (1835), which (as Madam de Stael pointed out) consists mainly of monologues and has few descriptive, dramatic, or con-textualising features, and links it more clearly with Boswell's method of dramatic presentation. Unlike Boswell, Eckermann has no grand formal idea governing his presentation of Goethe, and though (also unlike Boswell) his presence in the *Conversations* is transparent, the simplicity and fidelity of his style does transform the reader's perception of Goethe, as Boswell's *Life* does with Johnson. Eckermann's sensitivity to Goethe, and his conscious shaping comprehension of his material, is easily hidden by his stylistic simplicity, as in the following scene (11 April 1827):

I went to-day about one o'clock to Goethe, who had invited me to a drive with him before dinner. We took the road to Erfurt. The weather was very fine; the cornfields on both sides of the way refreshed the eye with the liveliest green. Goethe seemed as to his feelings gay and young as the early spring, but as to his words old in his wisdom.

'I ever repeat it,' he began, 'the world could not exist, if it were not so simple. This wretched soil has been tilled a thousand years, yet its powers are always the same; a little rain, a little sun, and each spring it grows green – and so it goes on.'

(*Conversations of Goethe with Eckermann*, trans. Oxenford (London, 1930), 186)

Eckermann uses the simplest, natural images and syntactical construction to invoke and embody Goethe's wisdom. He places Goethe in a setting that is at once natural and civilised (ancient cultivated cornfields), at once past, present, and future as nature unfolds itself in time (the wonders of the spring repeating themselves again and again). By contrasting and relating the natural details with Goethe's simple words of other-worldly detachment, Eckermann makes Goethe not only the centre of this eternal, feeling, natural moment, but its very creator and embodiment. Goethe's age reveals his youthfulness of spirit; his simple words record a respect for the rhythms of nature ('a little rain, a little sun, and each spring it grows green'), and they see into the mystery of life, which turns out to be as simple as the revelatory moment itself. Eckermann's passage conveys the profound simplicity of Goethe's character as it uncovers the profound simplicity of the world; and the depths of both are echoed in Eckermann's prose. There are many moments of this kind in the *Conversations*, exhibiting biographical and artistic capacities different from but akin to Boswell's.

Both Boswell and Eckermann artistically fashion conversation so that speech becomes a transparent medium in which the man's deeper character is embodied. Eckermann (1792–1854) met Goethe in 1823, when Goethe was seventy-four and, though active and lucid, coming to the end of his long and productive life in literature. Eckermann spent only nine years in Goethe's company, though the selectivity of the *Conversations* belies the amount of contact between the two men during that period. As with Boswell and Johnson, Goethe found in Eckermann someone whose soul was open to acts of extraordinary friendship: both biographers are highly sensitive and sympathetic, and enlist their need for romantic love in an artistic enterprise which effectively makes them not only the custodians but also the makers of the memories of the men they revered. Boswell's biography is a landmark not only because of its intrinsic qualities, its place in Enlightenment and proto-Romantic culture, but also because of its interesting connections with Eckermann's presentation of Goethe.

Conclusion: the place of the *Life*

The popularity of the *Life of Johnson* since its publication in 1791 is reflected in the number of editions. Croker's edition (1831) was the tenth, and though critics became sceptical of Boswell's methods in the mid-nineteenth century there were eleven major editions between 1874 and G.B. Hill's text in 1934, which (with L.F. Powell's revisions in 1950) has become standard.

Early readers testified to the success of Boswell's stated intentions. In 1792 William Elford wrote to Boswell: 'This kind of Biography appears to me perfectly new, and of all others the most excellent ... [for] instead of describing your characters, You exhibit them to the Reader. He finds himself in their company, and becomes an Auditor of Conversations' (*Corr.* 475). This view was echoed by other contemporary reviewers and in the very influential reviews of Croker's edition by Macaulay, Carlyle, and Lockhart. These nineteenth-century reviews were responsible for articulating the idea that Johnson was an eccentric, bigoted, yet 'great' man of moral energy whose fame was due to Boswell's portrayal rather than to his own writing. The idea that Johnson's interest lies primarily in his eccentric personality and its effect upon his writing has lasted down to the present day, constituting part of what Bertrand Bronson called the double tradition of Johnson, in which the 'popular' image of Johnson (mainly dependent on Boswell's account) ran side by side with a more scholarly understanding of Johnson based on his own writings. Yet, as Bronson recognises, the 'Boswell version' of Johnson has influenced the critical assessment of Johnson deeply. Many of the famous 'sayings' which characterise Johnson's presence and conversation in the *Life* have been revealed by Greene to be Boswell's own invention ('*Logia* of Johnson'). Among these is 'When a man is tired of London, he is tired of life; for there is in London all that life can afford.' Yet that precise formulation and many others like it are still doggedly identified not only as Johnson's words but among the statements that define who he is. This is a powerful, if flawed, legacy that Boswell has bequeathed to posterity.

At the same time Boswell's idiom was perpetuated throughout the nineteenth century into the twentieth because his biographical principles – especially his treatment of the significant particular and the dramatisation of the personality of the subject – were echoed and extended by Romantic aesthetics. There were many early nineteenth-century biographers and memoirists who imitated elements of Boswell's biographical method. Both Lockhart's *Life of Sir Walter Scott* (1837–8) and H.N. Coleridge's *Table Talk of the Late Samuel Taylor Coleridge* (1835) echo Boswell even while studiously denying direct imitation. Like Scott in his Lives of Dryden and of Swift, William Hazlitt's *Memoirs of the late Thomas Holcroft* (1816) use diary, letters, and other personal documentation popularised in Boswell's *Life*. Hazlitt's *Conversations of James Northcote* (1830) is explicitly inspired by Boswell's example. In the introductory note to the first six 'conversations' (originally planned under the title 'Boswell Redivivus'), Hazlitt astutely and mischievously identifies Boswell's central relationship with his subject in the process of identifying his own position: 'I differ from my great original and predecessor (James Boswell, Esq., of Auchinleck), in this, that whereas he is supposed to have invented nothing, I have feigned whatever I pleased. I have forgotten, mistaken, mistated, altered, transposed a number of things' (*Complete Works*, ed. P.P. Howe, vol. xi [1932], p. 350).

Hazlitt indicates one of the ways the Romantics were sympathetic to Boswell: they recognised that veracity did not exclude art. Though the early nineteenth century produced the cult of personality, with all its attendant opportunities for myth-making and sensationalism – exemplified in the commercially popular images of such people as Byron and Napoleon – biographers, such as Carlyle and Croker, realised that literal fact and truth were not identical, and that they were reconciled in the authentic artistic creation. Establishing authenticity as a touchstone of biographical form accepted the relativity of historical knowledge, and at the same time privileged the biographer's experience over fact. Samuel Pepys's diaries were published for the first time in 1825, coinciding with the interest in the artistically aware naive narrator, exemplified by Boswell. Romantic biography and aesthetics, therefore, extend and elaborate on Boswell's implicit interest in the biographer's subjectivity and how it contributes to the formal qualities of the text. Thomas de Quincey's *Literary Reminiscences* (1851) is, in this respect, perhaps the most Boswellian among Romantic biographies. This work acknowledges the inherent self-referentiality of literary biography. Boswell's pursuit and appropriation of Johnson, his mingled reverence and competitiveness, and his self-definition in the *Life*, are echoed by de Quincey in his relation to Wordsworth. But in de Quincey's case the biographer is rejected rather than welcomed by his subject. De Quincey is thereby able to dramatise his existential and social alienation more explicitly, but concomitantly is also able to generate his independence and personal artistic success more firmly.

Implicit in all of these Romantic biographers stands Coleridge's critical idea that 'sympathy' is of the essence of the artistic imagination, and Keats's belief that 'negative capability' (the capacity to enter into another's experience without any propensity to judge or rationalise it according to standards other than the immediately experiential) characterises the poetic sensibility. These were high Romantic virtues and seen as essentials for the successful biographer, as James Stanfield writes in his 'Essay on the Study and Composition of Biography' (1813). As applied to Boswell, all of these issues have become newly conceived commonplaces in the post-Malahide era — that is, since we have been able to see from Boswell's many manuscripts how conscientiously and deliberately shaping he was in his composition and how completely Boswell's Johnson is part of Boswell's Boswell. These have been the elements of Boswell's work that I have attempted to unfold in this book.

However, perhaps the most telling yet the most simple aspect of the 'afterlife' of the *Life of Johnson* is that it has been read by all who have the least curiosity about intellectual and moral character, and that its ambiguous and suggestive relation to Johnson himself has prompted students and scholars to return to it again and again, trying to clarify its pleasure and its meaning.

Bibliography and further reading

Boswell's works

The *Life of Johnson* appeared in 1791 in two volumes and went into a second edition in 1793 in three volumes. Edmond Malone helped Boswell throughout and edited the versions appearing in 1799, 1804, and 1811. J.W. Croker's edition of 1831 was the occasion of Macaulay's and Carlyle's famous reviews of the *Life*. The standard edition is *The Life of Samuel Johnson Together with Boswell's Journal of a Tour to the Hebrides*, ed. G.B. Hill, rev. L.F. Powell, 6 vols. (Oxford, 1934–64). More accessible is the World's Classics *Life*, ed. R.W. Chapman (rev. J.D. Fleeman), with an Introduction by Pat Rogers (Oxford, 1980 and 1987), from which I have quoted in this book.

Of Boswell's other works, relevant to the *Life*, the standard editions of *The Journal of a Tour to the Hebrides* are those in the Hill-Powell edition of the *Life*, and in the Yale Editions of Boswell's Private Papers (ed. F.A. Pottle and Charles H. Bennett (New York, 1961)). The Penguin edition is more accessible; it is published with Johnson's *Journey to the Western Islands of Scotland*, ed. Peter Levi (Harmondsworth, 1984). I have quoted from the first edition (1769) of *An Account of Corsica*, but a selection (*The Journal of a Tour to Corsica*; and *Memoirs of Pascal Paoli*) was edited by M. Bishop (London, 1951).

Boswell's papers were first edited and privately printed by Geoffrey Scott and F.A. Pottle as *The Private Papers of James Boswell from Malahide Castle*, 18 vols. (1928–34). Vol. VI deals with the making of the *Life*. The thirteen volumes of the 'trade edition', of the Yale Editions of the Private Papers is complete (1950–89) and published by McGraw-Hill (New York) and Heinemann (London). Christopher Morley's Preface to the *London Journal, 1762–63* (paperback, London, 1968) tells the romantic story of the discovery of the Boswell papers (1925–6, 1930–1). The 'research edition' of these papers (including Boswell's correspondence) has currently produced three volumes, and will be in progress for years to come. Some of Boswell's *Letters* have been edited by C.B. Tinker (Oxford, 1924).

The two main, complementary biographies of Boswell are F.A. Pottle, *James Boswell: The Earlier Years, 1740–1769* (New York, 1966), and Frank Brady, *James Boswell: The Later Years, 1769–1795*

(New York, 1984). Eighteenth-century biographies of Johnson include Hester Thrale Piozzi's *Anecdotes of Samuel Johnson, LL.D.* (1786) (excerpted in *Johnsonian Miscellanies*, ed. G.B. Hill (Oxford, 1897) – quoted here (*JM*)), and Sir John Hawkins's *The Life of Samuel Johnson, LL.D.* (1787). Hawkins's *Life* has been abridged by Bertram H. Davis (New York, 1961) – quoted here. Norman Page's *A Dr Johnson Chronology* (London, 1990) provides a detailed chronology of Johnson's life from day to day as well as brief biographical information on members of 'Johnson's circle'.

Other works by Boswell cited in this book are as follows:

The Hypochondriack, ed. M. Bailey, 2 vols. (Stanford, 1928).
On the Profession of a Player [3 Essays reprinted from *The London Magazine*, 1770] (London, 1929).
London Journal, 1762–1763, ed. F.A. Pottle (New York, 1950). [*LJ*].
Boswell for the Defence, 1769–1774, ed. W.K. Wimsatt and F.A. Pottle (New York, 1959).
The Correspondence and Other Papers ... Relating to the Making of the 'Life of Johnson', ed. Marshall Waingrow (New York, 1969). [*Corr.*].
Boswell in Extremes, 1776–1778, ed. C. McC. Weis and F.A. Pottle (New York, 1970).

Criticism

Criticism of *The Life of Johnson* and Boswell's life and other works increases steadily. There is a useful bibliography by John J. Burke in *British Prose Writers 1660–1800* that forms part of the *Dictionary of Literary Biography* (1991). The following is a list of works cited in this book, and a few others recommended to those wishing to further investigate the *Life* and its contexts:

Alkon, Paul, 'Boswellian Time', *Studies in Burke and his Time*, 14 (1973), 239–56.
Bogel, Fredric, *Literature and Insubstantiality in Later Eighteenth-Century England* (Princeton, 1984).
    'Did you Once see Johnson Plain?', in John Vance (ed.), *Boswell's 'Life of Johnson': New Questions, New Answers* (Georgia, 1985), pp. 73–93.
Brodwin, Stanley, ' "Old Plutarch at Auchinleck": Boswell's Muse of Corsica', *PQ*, 62 (1983), 69–93.
Bronson, Bertrand, *Johnson Agonistes and Other Essays* (California, 1965).
Carlyle, Thomas, 'Boswell's Life of Johnson', in *Critical and Miscellaneous Essays*, Vol. III (London, 1899).
Clark, J.C.D., *English Society 1688–1832* (Cambridge, 1985).

Clifford, James (ed.), *Twentieth-Century Interpretations of Boswell's 'Life of Johnson'* (Englewood Cliffs, 1970).

Clingham, Greg (ed.), *New Light on Boswell: Critical and Historical Essays on the Occasion of the Bicentenary of 'The Life of Johnson'* (Cambridge, 1991).

'Truth and Artifice in Boswell's *Life of Johnson*', in *New Light*, pp. 207–29.

Crawford, Thomas, *Boswell, Burns and the French Revolution* (Edinburgh, 1990).

Curley, Thomas, 'Boswell's Liberty-Loving *Account of Corsica* and the Art of Travel Literature', in Clingham, *New Light*, pp. 89–103.

Damrosch, Leo, *Fictions of Reality in the Age of Hume and Johnson* (Wisconsin, 1989).

Davis, Philip, *In Mind of Johnson* (London, 1989).

Dowling, William, *The Boswellian Hero* (Georgia, 1979).

'Boswell and the Problem of Biography', *Studies in Biography*, ed. D. Aaron (Cambridge, MA, 1978).

Language and Logos in Boswell's 'Life of Johnson' (Princeton, 1981).

Dwyer, John, *Virtuous Discourse: Sensibility and Community in Late Eighteenth-Century Scotland* (Edinburgh, 1987).

Greene, Donald, ' 'Tis a Pretty Book, Mr Boswell, But – ', in Vance, *Boswell's 'Life of Johnson'*, pp. 110–46.

'The *Logia* of Samuel Johnson and the Quest for the Historical Johnson', *Age of Johnson*, ed. Paul J. Korshin, Vol. III (New York, 1990), pp. 1–34.

Heiland, Donna, 'Remembering the Hero in Boswell's *Life of Johnson*', in Clingham, *New Light*, pp. 194–206.

Manning, Susan, *The Puritan–Provincial Vision* (Cambridge, 1990).

' "This Philosophical Melancholy": Style and Self in Boswell and Hume', in Clingham, *New Light*, pp. 126–40.

Macaulay, Thomas Babington, 'Samuel Johnson', in *Critical and Historical Essays*, Intro. by H. Trevor-Roper (New York, 1965).

'Life of Johnson' [for *Encyclopedia Britannica*], in *The Six Chief Lives from Johnson 'Lives of the Poets'*, ed. Matthew Arnold (London, 1934), pp. 1–45.

Morris, John, *Versions of the Self* (New York, 1966).

Nussbaum, Felicity, *The Autobiographical Subject* (Johns Hopkins, 1989).

'Towards Conceptualizing Diary', in *Studies in Autobiography*, ed. J. Olney (Oxford, 1988).

Parker, G. F., *Johnson's Shakespeare* (Oxford, 1989).

Pottle, F. A., *The Literary Career of James Boswell, Esq.* (Oxford, 1929).

'The *Life of Johnson*: Art and Authenticity', in Clifford, *Twentieth-Century Interpretations*, pp. 66–73.

Rader, Ralph, 'Literary Form in Factual Narrative: The Example of Boswell's *Johnson*', in Vance, *Boswell's 'Life of Johnson'*, pp. 25–52.

Schwartz, Richard, *Boswell's Johnson* (Wisconsin, 1978).

Scott, Geoffrey, 'The Making of the Life of Johnson as Shown in Boswell's First Notes', in Clifford, *Twentieth-Century Interpretations*, pp. 27–39.

Sher, Richard, *Church and University in the Scottish Enlightenment* (Princeton, 1985).

Siebenschuh, William, *Form and Purpose in Boswell's Biographical Works* (California, 1972).

Fictional Techniques and Factual Works (Georgia, 1983).

Simpson, Kenneth, *The Protean Scot: The Crisis of Identity in Eighteenth-Century Scottish Culture* (Aberdeen, 1988).

Spacks, Patricia Meyer, *Imagining a Self: Novel and Autobiography in Eighteenth-Century England* (Cambridge, MA, 1976).

Turnbull, Gordon, 'James Boswell: Biography and the Union', in *The History of Scottish Literature*, ed. A. Hook (Aberdeen, 1987).

Vance, John (ed.), *Boswell's 'Life of Johnson': New Questions, New Answers* (Georgia, 1985).

Waingrow, Marshall, 'Boswell's Johnson', in Clifford, *Twentieth-Century Interpretations*, pp. 45–50.